The Trees Around Us

The Trees Around Us

A Manual of
Good Forest Practice
For Nova Scotia

This Manual has been prepared on behalf of the
Provincial Forest Practices
Improvement Board in co-operation with the
Canada Department of Regional
Economic Expansion
and the Nova Scotia Department
of Lands and Forests.

ISBN 0-88871-004-6

Printed in Canada

A joint production of

 **Government
of Canada** **Gouvernement
du Canada** **Province of
Nova Scotia**

ACKNOWLEDGEMENTS

In the lengthy process of gathering new information and sharing the practical perceptions and judgements of Nova Scotians on the present state of the forests, cutting practices, and renewal of the forest resources to meet varied and increasing demands in this province, the consultant was privileged to have the hearty co-operation of knowledgeable individuals and organizations in all areas of forestry and the industry.

Numerous interviews, conducted throughout Nova Scotia during 1976-77 with persons in all aspects of forestry and the forest industry, provided the working basis for this Manual of Good Forest Practice for Nova Scotia, as well as the Forest Practice Guidelines to the Forest Improvement Act. It is the wish of the Provincial Forest Practices Improvement Board that this Manual be of practical value to Nova Scotia's thousands of private woodlot owners and operators, and that in a general way it will improve forest management and the forests of Nova Scotia.

The Board wishes to convey its gratitude to the Project Team which administered the preparation of the Manual. The Project Team engaged a consultant, W. S. Pollock, F. Eng., Timmerlinn Limited, Ste. Agathe Des Monts, Quebec, who researched and produced the initial textual material. The Nova Scotia artist, Paul Clarke, was commissioned to illustrate and design the book. An Editorial Committee was selected to transform the vast amount of material presented by the consultant into a concise Manual specifically related to Nova Scotia conditions.

The Board also expresses deep appreciation for the professional assistance of the Nova Scotia Department of Lands and Forests, the Nova Scotia Communications and Information Centre, the Nova Scotia Department of Development, and the Canadian Forestry Service; for permission to draw on materials published by the Faculty of Forestry, University of New Brunswick, and by the Forest Engineering Institute of Canada; and for the resources provided by numerous other organizations in Canada and the United States, as follows:

The Maritimes Forest Research Centre, New Brunswick Department of Natural Resources, Quebec Department of Lands and Forests, Quebec Department of Agriculture, Laurentian Forest Research Centre, Quebec; Ontario Ministry of Natural Resources, Great Lakes Forest Research Centre, Sault Ste. Marie; the Applied Forestry Research Institute, Syracuse, N.Y.; Northeastern Forest Experiment Station, Upper Darby, Penn.; Lake States Forest Experiment Station, St. Paul, Minn.; and Rocky Mountains Forest and Range Experiment Station, Fort Collins, Colorado.

FOREWORD

For many years, Nova Scotians have been aware of the need for intelligent action to help conserve our forests, in order to ensure future supplies of wood for the vital forest industry of this province and, at the same time, maintain the quality of the forest environment which is the protector of our wildlife, fresh water and recreation resources.

How to attack a problem of this magnitude was eventually resolved with improved data in forest management and fresh concepts arising from the sciences of forestry and ecology. In 1965 the Government of Nova Scotia enacted legislation, and by 1976 the present Forest Improvement Act was proclaimed.

The Act concerns better forest management for Nova Scotia, and is expected to encourage the continued renewal of the forests of this province for generations to come. The practical measures by which this may be achieved are spelled out in this Manual of Good Forest Practice for Nova Scotia. Advice and assistance in carrying out these measures, in many instances, is available through the Nova Scotia Department of Lands and Forests.

Under the Subsidiary Agreement for Planning, between the Canada Department of Regional Economic Expansion and the Government of Nova Scotia, preparation of the Manual was administered by a special Project Team consisting of forestry specialists and representatives from both levels of government.

Prepared for the use of Nova Scotia's thousands of woodlot owners and operators, foresters, technicians and other members of the forest industry, the Manual is considered essential to carrying out the intent of the Forest Improvement Act, and is expected to be of substantial assistance to those concerned with forest practices, particularly on private lands.

For supplementary information on the subjects covered in the Manual, selected publications are listed at the close of each chapter as suggested additional reading. Included in the appendices of the Manual are Forest Practice Guidelines which, after a reasonable test period, may form the basis for Regulations under the Forest Improvement Act.

CONTENTS

1
Our Forest Resources

The modern technology of this century gave the forest industry remarkable new tools which, somehow, led us to believe we were largely in control of the forest environment. In recent years, however, we have come to realize that any such control is very limited indeed. Faced with the true limitations of our technology, we can now identify basic rules of forestry which we have ignored at our peril — basic ecological rules. We understand today that we do not command the forest environment but are very much a part of it, and that what we do to the forest will sooner or later affect us. Slowly we are learning that we must work with nature, not against it. This means abandoning old habits of careless consumption, and adopting the wisdom of intelligent conservation.

Historically, the early settlers cleared and burned forests to make room for growing food and raising animals. They considered the forest an enemy. Later, the timber barons cut the best trees of the best species to create wealth, and the forest was assumed to be infinite and perpetual. More recently, amidst increased economic development and com-

petition, the demand for wood fibre has multiplied. As a result, the forests of Nova Scotia are certainly not what they used to be: Nova Scotians are faced with a potential shortage of softwood fibre, an over-abundance of unmerchantable hardwood, and forest stands of continuously declining vigour, quality and value.

Nevertheless, the trees and forests of Nova Scotia remain one of our most important renewable resources and, with adequate attention, we need never run out of supply. Like all living things, given a chance, the trees of the forest regenerate, mature, grow old and die. It is up to man to make use of them at an appropriate point in their life span and, most important, to ensure that they are replaced naturally by a new crop as good or better than the one that was cut.

This Manual outlines ways and means of accomplishing that goal. It is about good forest practice and management techniques which must now be undertaken if we are to re-establish a good quality forest resource that can be counted upon as a provider for the decades and the generations to come.

1

THE FOREST IMPROVEMENT ACT

The Manual of Good Forest Practice for Nova Scotia is authorized by Nova Scotia forest law, in the form of the Forest Improvement Act, Chapter 114 of the Revised Statutes of Nova Scotia 1967 (see Appendix I). The Act emphasizes maintenance, protection and rehabilitation of the forests, and productivity of the forest lands for the public welfare of Nova Scotia. Its stated objectives are: to provide supplies of forest products on a continuing basis; to sustain industry and provide employment; to conserve water and control floods; and to improve conditions for wildlife, recreation and scenic values.

In attempting to meet the requirements of the Forest Improvement Act, the manual deals particularly with four sections of the Act — though not exclusively. Moreover, guidelines have been adopted by the Provincial Forest Practices Improvement Board for these same four sections — sections 9 - 12 inclusive (see Appendix II).

Of the four sections specified, Section 9 deals with the felling of immature red and black spruce, pine, hemlock, and yellow birch; Section 10 concerns the felling of trees in accordance with recommended forest practice, including regeneration of desirable species; Section 11 has to do with the harvesting and utilization of all saleable wood from a stand; and Section 12 provides for greenbelts along designated highways, lakeshores and riverbanks.

INDUSTRY AND EMPLOYMENT

The combined value of pulp, paper and wood products in Nova Scotia makes up one third of the total value of all commodity exports from the province. Our forests currently support a modern manufacturing industry consisting of four pulp and paper mills, a hardboard mill, more than 300 sawmill firms and a large number of woodworking plants.

This industrial activity provides an estimated 4,500 full time jobs for Nova Scotians. Forest harvesting and related activities account for the equivalent of another 2,500 full time jobs, while a further estimated 18,000 jobs are indirectly related.

The magnitude of the forest products industry is reflected in the following figures on growth in production. Present statistics are available to 1976 only. In goods produced, the forestry sector of the Nova Scotia economy contributed in constant (1971) dollars $94.2 million in 1976, compared to $41.9 million in 1967.

Also expressed in constant (1971) dollars: the primary forest industry — logging — accounted for $8.6 million in 1976 compared to $6.4 million in 1967; while secondary processing — wood industries, pulp and paper, and allied industries — rose to $85.6 million in 1976 from $35.5 million in 1967.

In current dollars, the contribution to the provincial economy of the primary and secondary segments of the forest industry in 1976 totalled $152.1 million, in goods produced.

However, these figures represent only the dollar value of goods turned out by the industries producing, processing and utilizing wood fibre. The numerous other values of the forest to Nova Scotians cannot easily be expressed in terms of dollars and cents.

The forest not only supports thriving wood products industries, it is also the wildlife habitat of a wide variety of birds and animals. It reduces soil erosion and runoff, and protects the hundreds of rivers, lakes and

Oak Fruit (Acorn)

Red Oak

White Birch and Fruit

Red Maple and Fruit

streams which sustain fresh water game fish, feed hydro-electric power reservoirs, and provide major public water supplies.

Taken together, the forest, lakes and rivers provide many of the prime recreational resources — including provincial and federal woodland parks — which every year attract hundreds of thousands of vacationing Nova Scotians and visitors from other lands, who form the basis of our multi-million dollar tourism industry.

The value of the forest in terms of wildlife, recreation, water resources and the goods and services generated in relation to these, cannot be accurately quantified. Nevertheless, they are assigned an estimated annual value approximately equal to the goods producing industries of the forest. This figure would bring the total contributions of the forest to the provincial economy as high as twice the 1976 value of goods produced.

Thus, the forest as a whole is obviously greater than the wood products industry. It is a complex, living and renewable resource upon which a diversity of other resources, as well as industrial, commercial and recreational activities, depend. Indeed, the forest is one of the fundamental elements in the

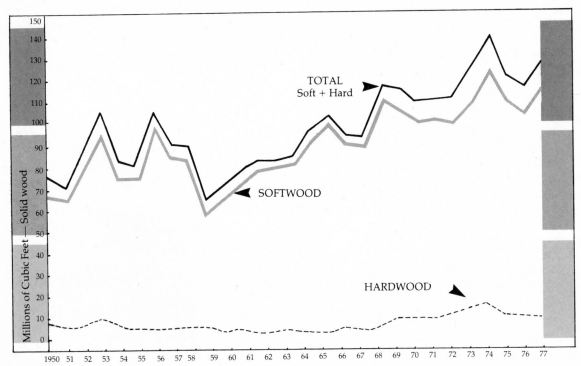

Growth Trend of Commercial Forest Production for Nova Scotia

precious quality of life, widely enjoyed in this province.

And therein lies the problem. Does enough wood exist in Nova Scotia to support the activities of our present forest industry over the long range and, at the same time, not dangerously interfere with the ecological balance of the forest environment, recreational usage, wildlife and other resources? Fortunately, the answer is a qualified Yes — provided all species and management inputs are considered.

OWNERSHIP AND PRODUCTION

Nova Scotia has a total of about 10.8 million acres (4.37 million hectares) of forest land. Of about 73 per cent in private ownership, 52 per cent is in small holdings of less than 1,000 acres (400 hectares). Land owned by the Nova Scotia government, and called provincial Crown land, comprises about 24 per cent, and three per cent is federal Crown land — owned by the government of Canada. This ownership pattern, showing a predominance of privately-owned forest land, is in sharp contrast to the general ownership pattern for all of Canada in which 92 per cent of all productive forest is Crown land.

About 10 years ago the small private ownerships produced around 60 per cent of the total wood harvest in Nova Scotia but this has dropped to about 40 per cent in recent years. Though the production from large ownerships and Crown land has made up for this decline, the present production level cannot be sustained without causing a shortage at some future date.

Today, many of the small ownerships are producing only a fraction of the yield they could produce in view of their relatively high capability and easy access. Moreover, it is well known that under good forest practice an average acre of Nova Scotia forest land can safely produce much more fibre than is grown at present.

FOREST CLASSIFICATION

Nova Scotia forests consist of about 53 per cent softwood stands, 30 per cent mixedwood and 17 per cent hardwood, according to the following classification:

Softwood - Stands containing 76 to 100 per cent softwood trees;
Mixedwood - Stands containing 26 to 75 per cent softwood trees;
Hardwood - Stands containing 25 per cent or less softwood trees.

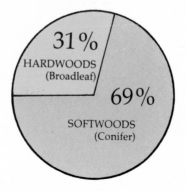

31%
HARDWOODS
(Broadleaf)

69%
SOFTWOODS
(Conifer)

Land Ownership in
Nova Scotia

(Water areas included in calculations)

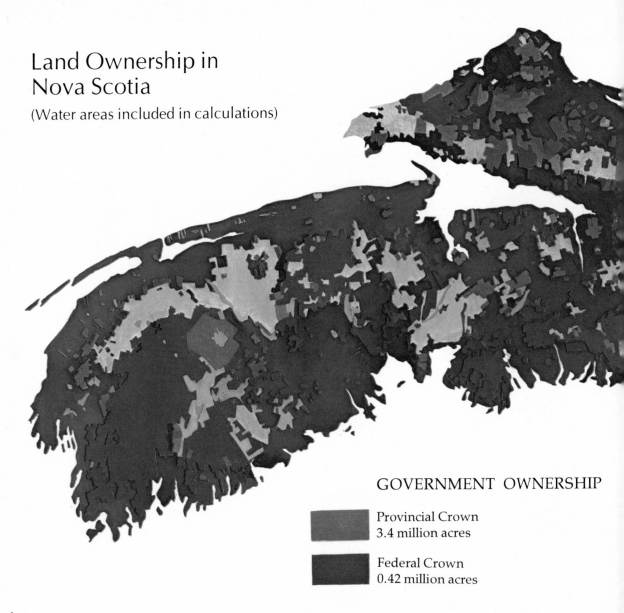

GOVERNMENT OWNERSHIP

Provincial Crown
3.4 million acres

Federal Crown
0.42 million acres

PRIVATE OWNERSHIP

 Small Private
(Less than 1,000 acres)

Small Private   7.4 million acres

 Pulp and Paper
Lumber
Other

Large Private   2.5 million acres

 Major Waterways

The Provincial Forest Inventory prepared by the Nova Scotia Department of Lands and Forests shows that softwood and hardwood species occur in Nova Scotia in the following order of relative abundance:

Softwoods	% Abundance
Red spruce }	
Black spruce }	27
Balsam fir	25
White spruce	7
White pine	5
Hemlock	3
Larch	1
Red pine	1
Totals	69

Hardwoods	% Abundance
Red maple	12
Yellow birch	6
Sugar maple	4
White birch	3
Trembling aspen }	
Large tooth aspen }	2
Beech	2
Red oak	1
White ash	1
	31

Recent inventory information also reveals that the gross merchantable volume of growing stock of all species is 9,904 million cubic feet (280 million cubic metres). Of this volume, 6,869 million cubic feet (194 million cubic metres) or 69 per cent is softwood and 3,034 million cubic feet (86 million cubic

Softwood   Hardwood

AGE CLASSES OF FOREST STANDS
Percent of total forested area

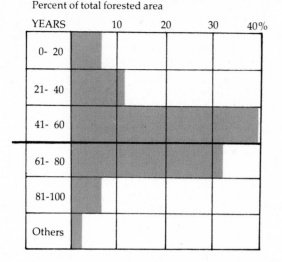

YEARS	10	20	30	40%
0- 20				
21- 40				
41- 60				
61- 80				
81-100				
Others				

DISTRIBUTION OF SIZE CLASSES
Percent of total volume of all species

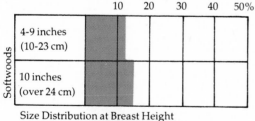

Softwoods

	10	20	30	40	50%
4-9 inches (10-23 cm)					
10 inches (over 24 cm)					

Size Distribution at Breast Height

Hardwoods

| 4-9 inches (10-23 cm) | | | | | |
| 10 inches (over 24 cm) | | | | | |

metres) or 31 per cent is hardwood. Of the gross merchantable volume, 22 per cent is on provincial Crown land, three per cent on federal Crown land, and 75 per cent is on private land.

The forest zone system provides a broad comparison of predominant tree species throughout the province (see map on page 10). Age classifications show a great deal of wood coming into the older age classes in the next 20 years, but there is little coming along to replace it (see age class chart, page 9). Of the total volume of all species in Nova Scotia, 25 per cent is in softwood species of a size suitable for sawlogs. In hardwoods, the figure is only 13 per cent and much of this will be of inferior quality for sawmill usage (see size class chart, page 9).

PRODUCTION CAPACITY

In the 25 years from 1935 to 1960, the average annual harvest in Nova Scotia was approximately 80 million cubic feet (2.26 million cubic metres). Since 1960 the annual harvest has increased rapidly, reaching 116 million cubic feet (3.28 million cubic metres) in 1977.

Meanwhile, sawmill production has declined steadily. In 1950 Nova Scotia sawmills produced about 350 million board feet per year, including 40 million board feet of hardwood. The 1977 volume was less than 200 million board feet, including only 10 million board feet of hardwood. During the same period the number of sawmill firms decreased from approximately 800 to around

FOREST ZONES OF NOVA SCOTIA

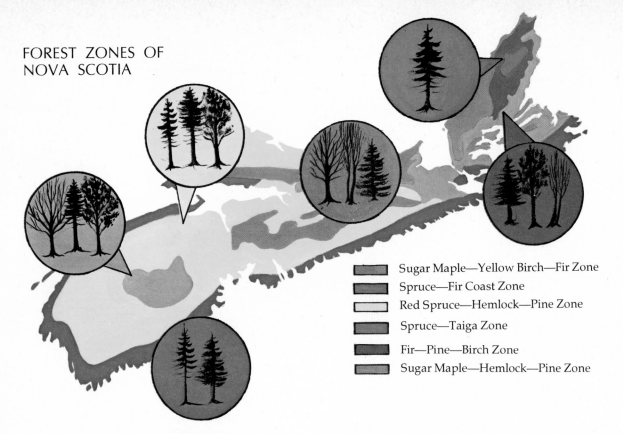

Sugar Maple—Yellow Birch—Fir Zone

Spruce—Fir Coast Zone

Red Spruce—Hemlock—Pine Zone

Spruce—Taiga Zone

Fir—Pine—Birch Zone

Sugar Maple—Hemlock—Pine Zone

300. However, there was a marked increase in the volume of pulpwood production.

Pulpwood constituted only 30 per cent of the total annual wood harvest before 1961. Since then two new mills opened, one at Point Tupper, the other at Abercrombie Point; followed by a hardboard plant at East River in 1967. All three of these mills expanded in the early 1970s. These industrial developments increased total pulpwood requirements to nearly 80 per cent of the total harvest. These and other factors since 1951 have brought about a 60 per cent decrease in the sawlog harvest and a 500 per cent increase in pulpwood harvest (see graph, page 11).

Using a simulation model, the Nova Scotia Department of Lands and Forests has calculated that the annual allowable cut is 136 million cubic feet, of which 98 million is in softwood species and 38 million in hardwood species. These estimates allow for accessibility, low density stands, small owner participation, waste and cull.

Production in 1974, the year which most closely represents industry capacity, was 135 million cubic feet, of which 121 million was

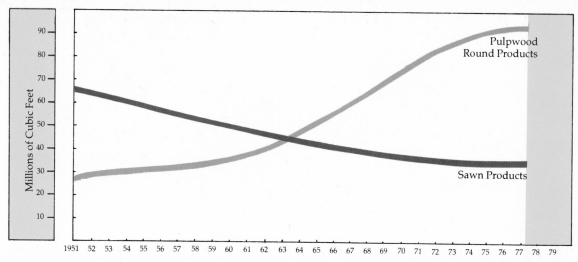

Annual Commercial Forest Harvest for Nova Scotia

softwood species and 14 million hardwood species. This indicates that softwoods are being overcut by 20 per cent and hardwoods undercut by 38 per cent.

On the optimistic side, however, is the capability of the forest to produce wood fibre. The average capability of forest land in Nova Scotia for timber production, assuming the proper species for the site and good management, has been estimated to be at least double the current annual growth.

It is estimated at present that an average acre of Nova Scotian forest land produces about 20 to 25 cubic feet per acre per year of wood fibre, but is capable of producing around 70 cubic feet per acre per year under good forest practice. Of course, not all stands grow at the same rate. Species and site conditions control growth but, where properly put into effect, good forest practice will improve forest growth. Thus, we must grow more high quality wood faster.

Additional Reading:

SAUNDERS, G. L. *Trees of Nova Scotia*. Truro, N.S.: Nova Scotia Department of Lands and Forests. Bulletin 37. 1973. 102 pages.

Nova Scotia Forest Inventory. Periodic subdivision reports and papers. Truro, N.S.: Nova Scotia Department of Lands and Forests.

Nova Scotia Forest Products Directory. An annual listing of producers and production of primary forest products. Truro, N.S.: Nova Scotia Department of Lands and Forests.

LOUCKS, O.L. *A Forest Classification for the Maritime Provinces.* Halifax, N.S.: Proceedings of the Nova Scotia Institute of Science. Volume 25, part 2. 1962. 167 pages.

Annual Reports — Nova Scotia Department of Lands and Forests. Halifax, N.S.: Queen's Printer, Province of Nova Scotia.

11

2
How Forest Stands Develop

Next to the lichens, mosses and ferns, trees represent the most ancient plant family living on earth. They also grow to the greatest age. Trees in some parts of the world grow to be several thousand years old, and even our own white pine may reach the advanced age of 450 years.

Soon after the glaciers of the last ice age retreated from the ancient coast of Nova Scotia, the first softwoods arrived — following the lichens and mosses northward as the ice melted. In the cool, moist climate of 11,000 years ago, our first known inhabitants, the Palaeo Indians, had sufficient spruce and fir for cooking fires, and for hafting spears and axes to hunt the caribou.

As the soil and climate improved over a period of several thousand years, pine, oak, beech and hemlock followed the early trees into Nova Scotia. Five thousand years ago — before the Pyramids arose or ancient Troy fell into ashes — our Indians of the Archaic

Four stages in the development of a softwood stand: from recent cutover (upper left) to the maturing next crop (lower right).

Period hunted game amid tall evergreen and hardwood groves, and fashioned canoes and cooking pots from the large boles of trees whose species are still common in Nova Scotia.

The forests and other vegetation which re-established in Nova Scotia and other parts of eastern Canada and the United States in the post-glacial period were never static in composition. Emerging from the vegetation south of New York and the Ohio Valley, which escaped the ice cap, our forests have altered in makeup over the millennia with the continuing changes in soil and climate.

These changes have been manifest in long-range ecological cycles of 2,000 to 3,500 years which have occurred with periodic alterations in moisture and temperature since the ice cap ceased to affect this region some 12,000 years ago. At present we are in a lengthy cycle of cool, moist climate favourable to maple, pine, hemlock and, of course, spruce and fir. If a dry, warm cycle occurs in the next few hundred years, it could encourage more oak and hickory — as it has before.

On the time scale of biological evolution, our softwood trees are far older than the hardwoods. In the Triassic Age of 200 million years ago, when tree-fern forests covered much of the earth, the coniferous trees evolved as strong competitors. Over 100 million years later the broad-leafed hardwoods emerged as dominant. This balance generally remains in effect today, except in northern climates and mountainous areas where the hardy softwoods have little competition.

In the process of re-establishing in this region during the post-glacial period, hardwoods followed the softwoods, forcing them to higher, rockier ground. Balsam fir, for example, belongs on the highland plateau of Cape Breton where it may survive a century of harsh mountain-top weather.

Throughout Nova Scotia, hemlock naturally belongs on the well-drained sites, and pine belongs to the sandy soils of western Nova Scotia. But there is very little left of what could be called virgin forest in the province. Much of our present softwood forest is established on former hardwood lands, cleared, burnt or cutover in the past century.

Of course, many natural factors, over which modern technology has little or no control, continually limit the growth, condition and composition of the forest. Our problems are not all due to adverse cutting practices. Wind storms, insect infestation, disease and forest fires are the great natural forces of change.

As long ago as 1802, Titus Smith was impressed with the vast acreage of windfallen trees in the mainland forest of Nova Scotia. The ravages of budworm have been the plight of the 1970s. But insect infestations, like the spruce budworm, and diseases, have always been with us. In the late 19th century, a sawfly attacking larch killed trees over large areas. Beech was dominant among the hardwoods until a parasitic fungus killed most of it earlier in this century. Birch briefly became dominant until birch die-back destroyed many of these trees, leaving maple dominant.

Cultural and economic patterns over the centuries also have had a profound effect on the growth of the forest, and continue to do so. Our Micmac Indians of historic times were members of the Abenaki whose flourishing eastern woodland culture probably began some 2,000 years ago. It was the Micmac who taught our early settlers the ways of the land and the forest. Homesteaders wresting farms from impenetrable forest hated it, but gradually changed their view with the advantages presented by the 19th century timber trade. Early land grants in this province helped direct the trade into private hands. Out of this arose Nova Scotia's great fleets of sailing ships, built from native woods, and trading goods around the world.

Highgrading for vessel construction and the timber trade removed the best trees of the best species from the forest. Meanwhile, many rural folk abandoned poor-paying farms to work in the mill towns, and in this century were followed by many others in the general shift from predominantly rural to urban life in Nova Scotia. Abandoned fields throughout the province produced young stands of white spruce, fir and larch. At the

A young softwood stand with an older stand in the background.

same time, the demand for forest products moved in the direction of greatly increased pulpwood production to supply the pulp and paper mills. But traditional inheritance patterns helped fragment, rather than consolidate, small woodland ownerships, and commercial forestry in Nova Scotia's vast number of small private holdings appeared relatively uneconomic. Current government programs are intended to help solve the problem. Thus, cultural and economic factors — as diverse as migrations, legacies, trade, technologies and legislation — also play vital roles in affecting the composition and growth of the forest.

FOREST STANDS

A forest consists of individual stands. A forest stand is a community of individual trees, sufficiently uniform in species composition, height, age, density and other conditions to be distinguishable from adjacent stands. Each stand occupies a specific area and reflects the period of time and circumstances under which the stand developed. Being recognizably different from one another, forest stands are the basic units for silvicultural treatments and the fulfillment of management objectives.

Forest stands may be even-aged, composed of trees with maximum age differences of 10 to 20 years; or uneven-aged, with considera-

15

ble age differences representing three or more age classes. They may have various heights and diameters, different site capabilities, high or low densities; be over or under stocked, stocked with a number of species or a single species, pure softwood or pure hardwood or mixtures of both; have high or low merchantable volume or none at all; be generally mature or immature or have trees of each in varying proportions, and so on.

As seedlings grow and develop in the stand they compete with one another for space, sunlight, moisture and food. Those on the best sites and with superior inherited qualities outstrip their neighbors to become the dominant and codominant trees of the stand. The suppressed trees are those that are pressed from the sides and over-topped by their neighbors. Between the suppressed and the codominants are the intermediates.

AGE AND GROWTH

From roughly the last of May to the first of August the cambium layer between the bark and wood produces a ring of wood cells which encircles the rootlets, the roots, the trunk or stem, the branches and the twigs.

The rapid growth of spring and early summer produces a band of light-coloured wood. A narrow band of darker wood is laid down during the slower growth of late summer and early fall. These two bands define the annual growth ring. The age of the tree can be determined by counting these rings.

Since it may be uncertain whether the smaller suppressed trees in a stand are younger or the same age as the larger ones, dominant and codominant trees are used to determine the average stand age. This age is one factor in determining immaturity under the guidelines to the Forest Improvement Act.

TREE DIAMETER

The average stand diameter is also used in determining immaturity under the guidelines to the Forest Improvement Act. Tree diameter increases with age as each annual ring is laid down, until growth ceases. If there is

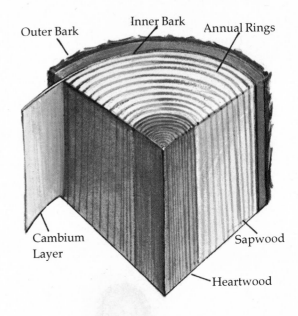

suppression from the sides or above, diameter growth is slow. If suppression is from one side only, diameter growth tends to become greater toward the open side.

Because of the varying degrees of suppression in stands, individual trees of the same age may have quite different diameters. A large tree is not necessarily an old one nor is a small tree always a young one.

It is not uncommon to find in large trees a small core, perhaps six inches in diameter, of closely packed annual rings, representing 150 years of suppressed growth. Upon release through partial cutting or some other cause, such trees have responded by increasing in diameter to as much as 12 or 14 inches over the next 30 years. Obviously, many years of diameter growth capability were lost during the first 150 years. Cleanings and thinnings would have produced more merchantable volume in a shorter time by allowing the trees to grow to the full capability of the site.

Measuring tree diameter (left) at breast height (DBH) with a tree caliper (see Line (4) page 40).

TREE HEIGHT

Under normal conditions, growth in height progresses at a rapid rate during the immature stages of trees. As a tree approaches maturity the rate of height growth decreases. Although greatly affecting diameter growth, suppression from the sides has little, if any, effect on height growth. Trees in a stand, with vigour to do so, will grow in height to the limit of the site capability. On better sites, trees will be taller at a given age than those on poorer sites.

STAND CAPABILITY

The quality of a forest site is rated by its ability to produce wood fibre in a given period of time. One purpose in rating the capability of the various stands in the forest is to establish silviculture and management priorities. The management of stands capable of producing the largest amounts of wood fibre annually should receive the most attention.

The average height growth at different ages of sample dominant and codominant trees can be used as an easy indicator of volume growth capability and, therefore, of stand capability. The relationships of height, at various ages in many sample trees, have been developed to show capability. An estimate of the age and the height from sample trees, may be used to determine the productive capability rating of a stand (see graph on page 18).

BASAL AREA AND DENSITY

The basal area of a tree is the area in square feet of the cross section of the tree at breast height. The stand basal area is the total area of the cross sections of all trees on an acre. The

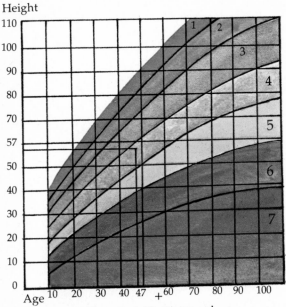

Height

Forest capability rating of Dominant and Codominant trees based on Nova Scotia Yield tables

Graph shows forest capability rating of dominant and codominant trees based on Nova Scotia yield tables. For example, a 47-year-old stand having an average height of 57 feet will have a capability rating of 4, and be able to produce up to 70 cubic feet of wood per acre per year (see Line (7) page 41).

INTERMEDIATE

SUPPRESSED

DOMINANT   CODOMINANT

Trees for age/height study

basal area may be the same for a stand of many small trees as for one with a few large trees. A very small proportion of a stand is occupied by tree stems. Hence, basal area per acre is a true indicator of the proportion of the area occupied by trees. As such, it is a true measure of stand density and, along with height, is used in estimating volume.

A normal stand is one with a closed crown cover, with neither wasted space nor suppression through overcrowding. In a high density stand, the crown cover is so completely closed that the tree crowns suppress one another. In a low density stand the crown cover is open.

The relationship between crown closure and basal area is a practical aid for determining density. An estimate of the percentage of crown closure may be used as an indicator of density, just as the actual measurement of basal area is a measure of density.

Because basal area may be made up of many small trees or relatively few large ones, it is important to know the stocking conditions as well. Taken together, stocking and density help in making management decisions.

Dominant trees have well developed crowns and rise above the general level of the crown cover in the stand. Receiving full light from above and some from the sides, they grow larger than other trees in the stand. Condominant trees form the general level of the crown cover. With full light from above but comparatively little from the sides, the codominant trees are somewhat smaller and have medium-sized crowns.

NUMBER OF TREES, OR STOCKING

A stand may begin with a few, or tens of thousands of trees per acre. If there are only a few trees per acre, widely spaced, or if there are thousands in scattered clumps, the stand will be understocked. During the development of natural stands, from many seedlings per acre, suppressed trees and others die, and the crowns of the more dominant trees grow to fill the vacated spaces. The number of trees per acre decreases naturally with age.

The full capability of a site can be realized only if each tree has enough space for adequate crown development. Each tree requires only a certain space in which to develop an ideal crown. If a stand is overstocked the crowns are suppressed, as is diameter growth; consequently, years of growth are wasted. If understocked, on the other hand, trees will tend to fill the space with deep, spreading crowns and space is wasted.

Thus, at a given age and with a given site capability, for each stand there is an ideal number of trees per acre. Such a condition is known as normal stocking. The better the capability rating, the fewer trees required to provide normal stocking.

A nicely closed stand may occur with 520 trees per acre at 60 years on one site, while on a poorer site such a stand would be very open. Also, an ideally closed stand may occur with 1,020 trees per acre in one case, while on a better site this same stocking would cause crowded conditions.

Although overstocking will suppress the diameter growth and increase the crown closure of trees in a stand, it has little effect on height growth which will progress at a rate determined by site capability.

VOLUME PER ACRE

A tree accumulates volume by the addition of each annual growth ring from its base to its tip. The rate of volume growth increases rapidly during the immature stages of a tree, reducing towards maturity, until it ceases. The volume of a tree is determined from basal area and height, and stand volume per acre is simply the total of individual tree volumes.

Age, diameter, height and basal area are readily measured or calculated. Tree and stand volumes are not so easily obtained by direct measurement. Various kinds of volume and yield tables are used to estimate volumes per acre from direct measurements of sample trees and plots. Such tables are constructed from accumulated detailed measurements of many felled trees, and plot studies.

It is difficult to present satisfactory general merchantable volume tables for standing trees, due to varying degrees of utilization. Because trees and stands have a variety of uses, the amount of wood fibre in a tree or stand depends on the volume that can be used. An overstocked, very dense sapling stand may have significant volume for bean pole or palisade fence uses, but not have one stick of pulpwood.

Another less heavily stocked and less dense stand may have a very high pulpwood volume but not a single sawlog. With less stocking and lower density, in a third stand there may be a high sawlog volume on uniform trees with optimum diameters for the site and age. Thus stand volumes may be expressed as follows:

Gross Volume per Acre: is the measure of total wood volume in cubic feet of the entire stems, including stumps of all the trees 1.6 inches in diameter at breast height (DBH) and larger. This may be called 100 per cent of the wood fibre yield.

Gross Merchantable Pulpwood Volume per Acre: represents the solid wood portion in cubic feet of the gross volume, above a specified stump height, used as 4-foot pulpwood to minimum top diameters of 3.6 inches inside bark. This represents about 75 per cent of the gross volume of stands on average sites at 60 years of age.

Gross Merchantable Sawlog Volume per Acre: means that portion in feet board measure of the gross volume above a specified stump height, used as an average log length of 12 feet (none less than eight feet) to minimum top diameters of 5.6 inches inside bark. In practice, it usually applies to trees larger than eight inches DBH for softwoods and 10 inches DBH for hardwoods. This is only about 45 per cent of the gross volume of stands on average sites at 60 years of age.

Net Merchantable Volume per Acre: refers to the remainder of the gross merchantable volume for pulpwood and for sawlogs after estimated deductions for unusable species, cull and defects have been made.

THE ANNUAL YIELD

Merchantable volume accumulates slowly or not at all in the early stages of stand development, more rapidly in the middle and toward the maturing stages. The time between the removal of one mature crop and the harvest of the next mature crop is called the rotation. This varies with species and growing conditions, such as site, density and stocking, as well as the product planned — a shorter time for pulpwood and longer for saw timber.

Throughout the total rotation there are drains on yields, offset to varying degrees by gains. Drains may be caused by such things as insects, cutting, thinning; gains are the result of growth. The balance at any given time is the inventory of growing stock volume which, divided by the age at that time, gives the average annual yield. Whether the yield is merchantable in size depends on the age and growing conditions.

If most of the stands in any woodlot are in immature age classes, there will be a waiting period for merchantable volume to develop. On the other hand, if most of the acreage is in mature and overmature age classes, it may be desirable to cut heavily to reduce the losses from decadence. Of course, this will mean cutting less wood later.

Ideally, there should be a balance of age classes to provide for annual or periodic harvest on a continuing basis. This can be achieved in a regulated forest and is an ultimate goal of forest management. It calls for cutting the proper amount of wood in the proper place at the proper time.

Calculating the annual allowable cut by

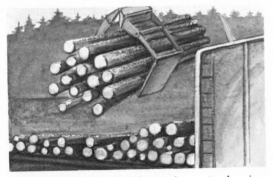

Eight-foot pulpwood is loaded crosswise on a truck, using a hydraulic loader.

Because of their length, sawlogs are loaded lengthwise. Hydraulic loaders frequently are mounted behind the cab.

volume to balance out the drains and gains and, at the same time, working towards a regulated forest, is not a simple exercise. Nevertheless, such a calculation does provide a rough guide which can be followed reasonably closely, not necessarily annually, but perhaps over a five year period and certainly over a ten year period. A periodic reassessment of the inventory will reveal whether the growing stock volume has been over or under cut and adjustments made for the next period.

IMMATURITY

The Forest Improvement Act defines an immature stand as, "an area of not less than three acres of young healthy spruce (red and black), pine, hemlock or yellow birch which according to the criteria established as a result of studies carried out by the Minister pursuant to subsection (3) of Section 9 is an immature stand."

Trees and even-aged stands go through four stages of growth: (a) an initial period of seedling and sapling development, (b) a middle period, (c) the period of maturity, and (d) the period of decline.

During the initial period of development there is no merchantable volume. In the middle period annual merchantable volume growth increases at a rapid rate. Volume growth increases slowly during the period of maturity until losses exceed sound growth in the period of decline.

The yearly increase in growth is known as the Current Annual Increment (CAI). This is

Stages of growth

Stages of growth

Initial period
Middle
Maturity
Decline

Increment Core

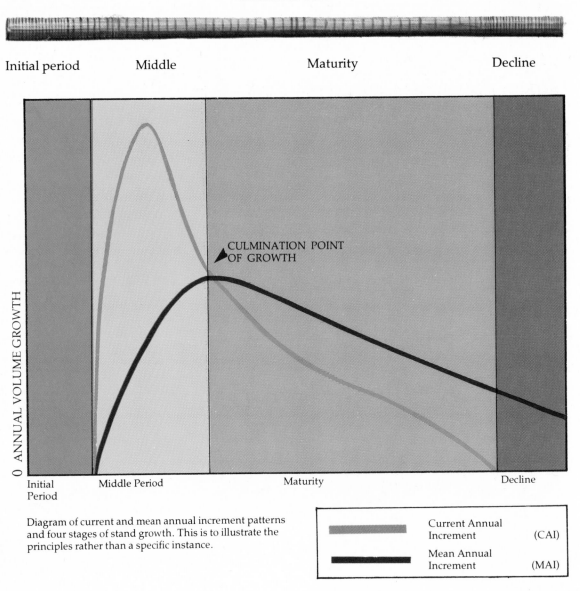

Initial period   Middle   Maturity   Decline

CULMINATION POINT OF GROWTH

0 ANNUAL VOLUME GROWTH

Initial Period   Middle Period   Maturity   Decline

Diagram of current and mean annual increment patterns and four stages of stand growth. This is to illustrate the principles rather than a specific instance.

	Current Annual Increment (CAI)
	Mean Annual Increment (MAI)

24

usually measured as the average yearly growth over a period of 10 years. The volume of the stand at any given time divided by its age at that time is known as the Mean Annual Increment (MAI) (see graph on page 24).

MAI continues at lower levels than CAI even for a time after CAI is decreasing. As the stand approaches maturity CAI continues decreasing and falls below MAI. When the two are equal — at the culmination point of growth — the stand is regarded as being at the peak of average yearly volume growth. The stand volume continues increasing slowly to the period of decline when CAI becomes less than the losses through decadence.

Subsections (2) and (3) of Section 9 of the Act refer to a satisfactory criterion of economic culmination and growth on average stands at which the peak of potential yield or volume can be expected, or the stage of growth at which a given acre will, on the average, produce the greatest volume of wood. A program of permanent plot remeasurements is under way to help define this criterion.

Meanwhile, in the absence of something better, alternative guidelines are proposed for judging immaturity. The following discussion is background to the development of these guidelines to Section 9 of the Act (see Appendix II).

For various purposes, an overall average rotation age of 70 years is suggested for stands in Nova Scotia. This is based on: (a) 40 to 60-year rotations for pulpwood and shorter-lived species, and (b) 70 to 100 year rotations for sawlogs and longer-lived species. These ages are based on free growth without any suppression from overcrowding, and no loss of time in the establishment of regeneration. Assuming it takes an average of 10 years for seedlings to grow to breast height, the average rotation age would be 60 years for trees measured at breast height.

Earlier yield table studies by the Department of Lands and Forests indicate an average tree diameter of six inches for average stands at this 60 year rotation age. This is based on all stems 1.6 inches diameter and up at breast height. Excluding those trees below merchantable size — less than 3.6 inches DBH — the average tree diameter may be taken as seven inches.

The Provincial Forest Practices Improvement Board has accepted, for the purpose of the Act, an immature stand of desirable species as one:

1 not less than 3 acres in size;
2 consisting of vigorous and healthy trees of an age, height, species make-up and density, and different with respect to these features from surrounding forests;
3 with more than 50 per cent of the volume in red or black spruce, pine, hemlock or yellow birch, or mixtures of these species; and
4 falling into one of the following:
   (a) less than 60 years of age at breast height;
   (b) having an average stand diameter of less than seven inches DBH.

This is a general guide by which to decide whether a stand is immature. If by these guidelines a stand appears to be immature, it should receive the attention of the Board before being cut. On the other hand, if a stand is not immature by these guidelines, it may be cut without the permission of the Board. This is not to imply that it is a mature stand and should be cut. There are indicators of maturity which can be used in making this decision, such as:

1 Sharp reductions in widths of annual rings for at least the last 10 years, as compared with the best 10 years in dominant and codominant trees, may indicate stand maturity.

2 Rounded tips of softwood trees, because of reduced height growth for some years, may indicate maturity.

3 Decadence, as evidenced by dead twigs and branches and thinning foliage in the upper crown, may be a further indication of maturity if it has been going on for several years from other than a recognized temporary cause.

4 Well established regeneration, that can be expected to produce a desirable stand after logging, is another indication that nature has prepared the way for removal of the old stand.

Red Spruce   Black Spruce   White Pine

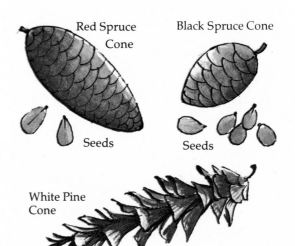

Red Spruce Cone   Black Spruce Cone

Seeds   Seeds

White Pine Cone

Red Pine   Hemlock   Yellow Birch

Red Pine Cone and Seeds

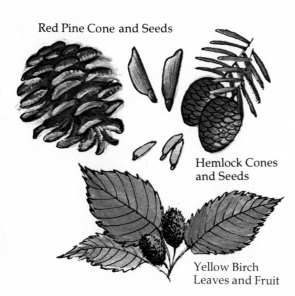

Hemlock Cones
and Seeds

Yellow Birch
Leaves and Fruit

The principles of growth and yield of trees and forest stands are basic to good forest practice. The Department of Lands and Forests has demonstrated that by manipulating stocking and density through planting, cleaning, thinning and improvement cutting, average annual yields can be increased both by volume and quality whether for pulpwood or saw timber or both. Improved utilization over the lifetime of a stand, as well as at harvest, will lessen the differences between merchantable and gross volumes, and increase yields.

Additional Reading:

BICKERSTAFF, A. and S. A. HOSTIKKA. *Growth of Forests in Canada*. Ottawa, Ont.: Canadian Forestry Service. Forest Management Institute. Information Report FMR-X-98. 1977. 197 pages.

DONALDSON, J. *The Pulp Industry in Nova Scotia*. Truro, N.S.: Nova Scotia Department of Lands and Forests. 6 pages.

FERGUSON, B. *Lumbering in Nova Scotia: 1632-1953*. Truro, N.S.: Nova Scotia Department of Lands and Forests. 25 pages.

HAWBOLDT, L.S. and R. M. BULMER. *The Forest Resources of Nova Scotia*. Truro, N.S.: Nova Scotia Department of Lands and Forests. 1958. 171 pages.

SMITH, TITUS. *A Natural Resources Survey of Nova Scotia, 1801-1802*. Truro, N.S.: Nova Scotia Department of Lands and Forests. 40 pages.

SPURR, S. H. and B. V. BARNES. *Forest Ecology*. New York, U.S.A.: The Ronald Press Company. 1973. 570 pages.

WILSON, B. F. *The Growing Tree*. Amherst, Mass., U.S.A.: University of Massachusetts Press. 1970. 152 pages.

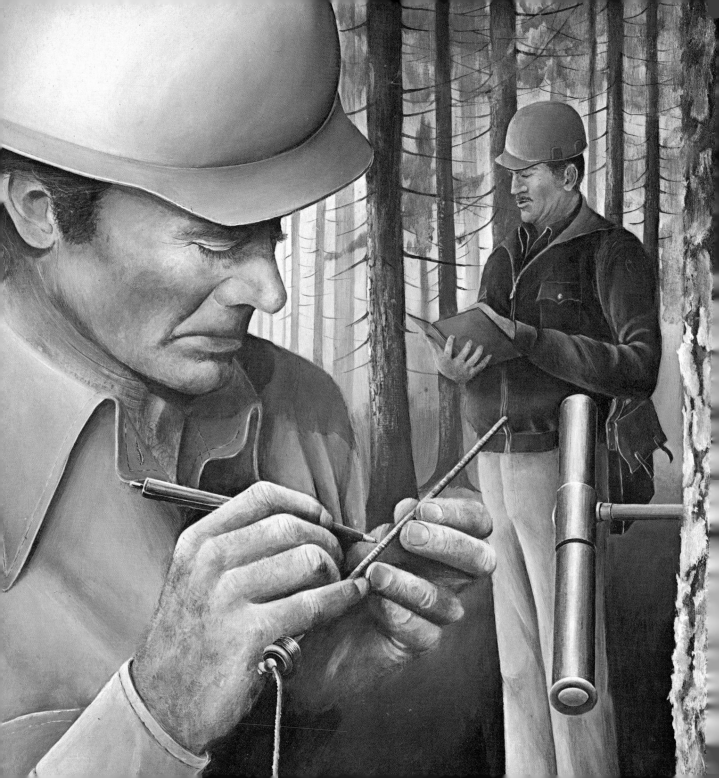

3
Forest Management Planning

A forest management plan will show the parts of your forest where you should carry out harvest cutting, how it should be done, and what the harvest may yield. It will also indicate where access roads are needed to carry out cultural and harvesting operations; the stands requiring silvicultural work and the kind of treatment — cleaning, thinning or planting; it will show where fire ponds are advisable, and may include recreational improvements and other recommendations. The forest management plan, prepared by a private land forester, is based upon:

An inventory of the forest land which will provide information on what you have in terms of stands — their ages, species composition, density, height, volume and quality.

Obtaining the age of a tree (left) by counting the annual rings on an increment core.

You must also know the location of these stands in relation to property boundaries and roads. This requires a map showing all the different stands. The forest inventory and stand map are required for any rational future use of your forest. No one can properly manage a piece of forest land without knowing what is growing on it. The forester will consider the land capability and the market potential for products in making recommendations.

The landowner's objectives for his forest land are just as important as the forest inventory. What you, the landowner, undertake in the forest depends upon your objectives, provided they are compatible with the forest, site, climatic and economic conditions. Forests may be wanted for fibre production, income, employment, wildlife, recreation or water conservation, or combinations of these and other uses. Certain objectives may apply only to specified portions of the property. Management treatments will differ for various objectives and, indeed, may appear to conflict as a result of incompatible objectives.

For example, a forest of one species of the same age would generally be unfavourable for scenic and wildlife objectives. A hardwood forest kept as low sprouts would be valuable for deer browsing but useless for timber, recreation or scenic values. A forester can help you determine whether your objectives are in harmony with the ecological realities of the forest, the requirements of the Forest Improvement Act, and the social and economic conditions of your community.

The owner's objectives can be viewed in terms of values, tangible and intangible, which he would like to obtain from his forest land. What values can be realized from forest management? Personal satisfaction may be of prime importance to the absentee owner of a small, easily accessible property close to an urban area, particularly if his income is not derived from ownership of that land. The motivation of many absentee owners, with large acreages in remote areas, may also be largely personal satisfaction. Other owners, however, may put financial returns ahead of personal satisfactions. This will likely be the case with most resident farmer owners whose woodlands are part of the farm. Finally, there are those who want a combination of personal satisfaction and financial return.

The proposals of a management plan will depend upon the nature of your forest property and what you want from it. If you have a great deal of over-mature timber and want a financial return, the plan will outline the cheapest and most efficient way of harvesting this timber and successfully establishing a new stand in its place. If you own cutover land and want to improve it with the aid of a government program, the plan will outline the most important areas to be treated and explain how to go about it. Some programs require that you have a plan before you can obtain assistance.

The owner's attitude towards various forestry activities is also important. For instance, you may favour planting trees and prefer the planting of single species, or desire a more diversified plantation with a variety of

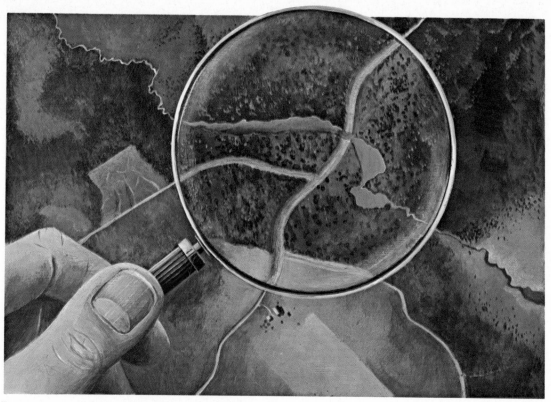

Examining an aerial photograph with the enlarged section seen through a magnifier.

species. If the stand is suitable for clearcutting, do you want clearcutting? If not, a form of partial cutting is in order. Of course, it is your responsibility to relate these attitudes and wishes to the forester or forest technician who draws up your management plan.

GROUP MANAGEMENT

Small or narrow properties and those of irregular shape are difficult to manage. Group management is a term used to describe a situation where a number of property owners get together to form an association for forest management and marketing purposes.

One of the biggest advantages of group management is that silvicultural crews can be trained and have continuous work on all the properties in the group. Where the properties are adjacent to one another, less expensive road networks may be planned to cross properties, rather than each property having to be serviced individually. If sufficient land is owned by members of the group, a forester or forest technician may be hired by the group as a manager.

MAPPING THE FOREST

No matter what you plan for your woodland, a map of your property is essential. The most accurate boundary map is one prepared by a land surveyor. Just as essential, however, is knowing your boundary lines on the ground.

It is a good policy to mark your boundary lines with paint at breast height every five years or so. This will be easily seen by your neighbour in the event that he cuts wood close to your line. Whatever you do, don't build roads or cut any trees unless you are certain you are on your own land.

If you are uncertain of your lines, you should hire a registered Nova Scotia land surveyor. A list of qualified land surveyors is available from the Association of Nova Scotia Land Surveyors or from the Department of Lands and Forests. Your forester or forest technician will be able to offer you advice on

Blazes painted on trees mark property boundary lines. Wooden cornerposts with numerical inscriptions are being succeeded by identifying metal rods driven into the ground.

boundary line maps for your property (a table of map scales and conversions appears in Appendix III).

Once you have located your property on a map you can order a set of colour or black and white aerial photographs at a scale of 1:15,850 or 1:10,000 as available. Photographs may be purchased from the Maritime Resource Management Service in Amherst, N.S. Send them the map of your property on a Forestry Base Map or Topographic Map, and request full stereoscopic coverage of your property. These photographs can be used by a forester or forest technician to draw a forest stand map of your property. The various forest stands identified are marked directly on the air photograph in black ink.

Forest typing on aerial photographs is done with the aid of a stereoscope and requires a pair of photographs with an overlap of about 60 per cent from one photograph to the next (see illustration on page 31). The stereoscope gives the viewer a three dimensional view of the property. The trees and forests appear to stand up above the ground in relief. The stereoscope also aids the viewer in distinguishing forest cover types. A good photo-interpreter may identify individual species from the photographs, estimate stand heights, stand density and may sometimes identify forest capability and soil classes.

Once you have a forest map of your property showing the various forest stands, you will want to know and record the area of each stand. The simplest way to do this is with a dot grid.

A dot grid is a sheet of clear plastic with one

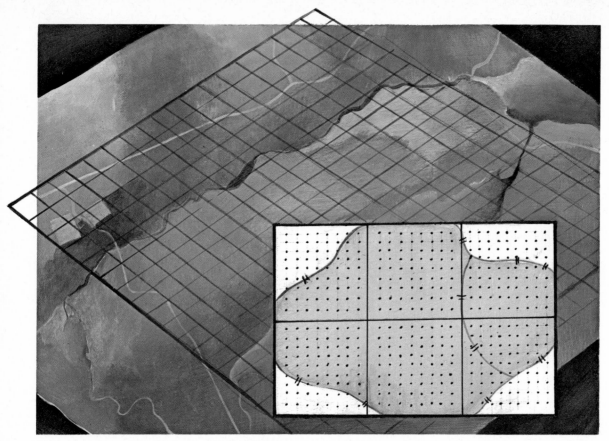

Dot grid overlaying an aerial photograph. The enlarged section over the forest stand shows the dots to be counted in determining the area of the stand.

inch (centimetre) squares on it. Inside the squares are a number of dots. Each dot represents a certain number of acres (hectares), according to the map scale. By counting the dots which fall on a particular forest stand when the grid is placed over the map, and multiplying this dot count by the number of acres (hectares) each dot represents at that scale, the total acreage is estimated. Dots which fall on a forest stand boundary, should be counted as one-half dot, or you may count every other one, for an accurate total.

If no trees were cut following aerial photography, the photographs should provide for satisfactory classification of your forest into forest stands for management planning purposes. If cutting was carried out since the photos were taken, the cutover areas should be mapped as well as any new roads and skidding trails. To do this you will require a base map, a mapping compass, pencil and clipboard.

The procedure is to determine the direction with the compass and the length by pacing off each segment of the old and new road as accurately as possible, and plot them consecutively on the base map in their correct relative positions. Measuring distance by pacing, rather than by using a surveyor's tape or

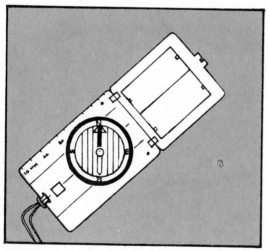

Hand-held mapping compass commonly used in forestry. In addition to the floating needle, a directional arrow may be rotated with the case. A distance scale is inscribed on one side of the base, and a cover closes to protect the compass face.

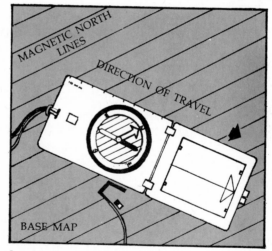

In using the mapping compass, the arrow is set at magnetic north, parallelling magnetic north lines drawn on the base map. The angle between arrow and compass needle marks the direction of travel (see page 36).

chain, is very useful. In the woods, most people have a pace (of two steps) measuring about five feet (1.5 metres). To determine the length of pace, practice pacing a known distance, and divide this distance by your number of paces.

Let's say you want to map the location of a new road you have just built. First draw parallel lines about one inch apart on the map, corresponding to the direction of magnetic north. Mark a point on the base map as your starting point, as close as possible to the beginning of the new road you want to map.

Beginning at your starting point, pace along the road to the point where the new road forks off from the one on your map. Using the ruler on the compass, and the map scale, mark the distance on the base map. This is where the new road starts. Now, take a compass bearing down the new road on the first segment, or to the point where the road begins to take its first turn. Without moving the compass case, lay the compass on the map so that the north arrow (not the magnetic needle) and the lines inside the compass case, are parallel to the magnetic north line on the map and pointing towards magnetic north. The side of the compass base plate should run through the point on the map where the road forks. Draw a line from this point to represent the direction of travel along the new road. Now, pace the distance and mark off this distance at the appropriate scale on your map along the direction-of-travel line you have drawn. You are now at the end of the first segment.

A stereoscope for three-dimensional viewing of a pair of aerial photographs.

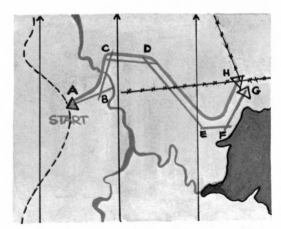

Mapping road by means of a mapping compass and pacing, starting at point A and ending at G, with a tie to H.

36

Do each segment of the road in the same manner. Eventually you will have a map of the road (see illustration on page 36). It is a good idea, when you reach the end of the road, to tie in the location with another known point on the property by measurement and bearing. As you map the road you can also indicate on the map the approximate location of streams, forest type changes, lakes and other features. If you are mapping cutover areas, you need only map the roads and skidding trails, since the boundaries of the cutover can be estimated from the ends of the skidding trials.

CRUISING YOUR FOREST

In forestry, the word "cruise" is used to describe the activity of carrying out a forest survey to estimate the quantity (volume) of wood in forest stands, according to species or species groups, age, size, quality, possible products and other characteristics.

Once you have a forest stand map, you need to learn more about the actual condition of each stand, the volume of merchantable wood each contains, the proportion of hardwood and softwood, conditions for regenera-

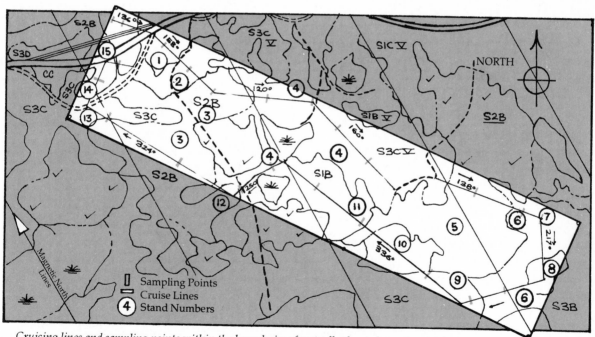

Cruising lines and sampling points within the boundaries of a woodlot located on a forest type map.

tion, whether or not the stands are immature, their capability to produce forest products, and whether or not the stands require silvicultural treatments.

Many landowners prefer to have a private land forester or forest technician cruise their property for them. The Department of Lands and Forests employs a number of private land foresters and technicians who are available through each subdivision to assist landowners in woodlot management. The stand descriptive cruising method of obtaining information about forest stands for management planning is outlined below so that you will know what is involved in a forest cruise and how the data is gathered.

In stand descriptive cruising, each stand must be visited and described and special measurements of trees made. Special tools are required, including an increment borer, clinometer, a wedge prism and a tree caliper. To locate more remote stands, pace with a compass. When you are sure you are in the right stand, tie some plastic flagging ribbon around a nearby tree, to mark the stand and proceed with the measurements described in the following pages.

In cruising, two steps equals one pace — about five feet — (see page 35).

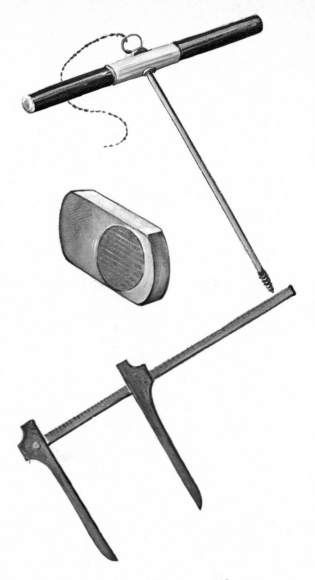

Tools used in descriptive cruising: increment borer (top), clinometer (centre), tree caliper (bottom).

Woodland Management Stand Assessment Sheet

1.	Line number or Bearing				
2.	Stand number				
3.	Area				
4.	Average Diameter				
5.	Average Age				
6.	Average Height				
7.	Forest Capability				
8.	Maturity				
9.	Density				
10.	Drainage				
11.	Windfirmness				
12.	Species Composition				
13.	Cover type				
14.	Wildlife Habitat Features				
15.	Products				
16.	Treatments				
17.	Priority				
18.	Average Stand Basal Area				
	Basal Area Desirable Species				
19.	Gross Merchantable Volume				
	Total				
	Pulpwood: SW				
	HW				
	Sawlogs: SW				
	HW				
	Desirable Species only				
20.	Non-merchantable Volume: SW				
	HW				
21.	Regeneration				
	Species Composition				
	Stocking				
	Height				

RECORDING STAND DESCRIPTIONS

The assessment sheet is used to record all the descriptive information for the different stands in your forest. The lines on the sheet are numbered to help explain the required information and its use, and the various classes are coded by number. One column on each part of the sheet is used for each stand on your property.

Line (1) is used to record the compass bearing or cruise line number used to reach the stand. This provides a record of the location where your sampling was done.

Line (2) indicates the stand number. The numbers should be consecutive. Make sure the number on the map corresponds to the number on the sheet and be certain you mark the number on the map.

Line (3) concerns the area of the stand in acres (hectares). This comes from your area calculations using the dot grid (see page 34).

On Line (4) record the average diameter in stands that contain more than 50 per cent of their volume in desirable species. See Line (19) first, to determine if you have the required volume in desirable species.

The guidelines to Section 9 of the Act (Appendix II) recommend four 1/10 acre (66 feet × 66 feet) plots per stand be measured, one in each quarter of the stand. With a tree caliper, measure all trees of all species larger than 3.5 inches (nine centimetres) in diameter at breast height, that is 4.5 feet (1.3 metres)

above the ground, inside each 1/10 acre plot. Measure each tree to the nearest one inch (two centimetres) and calculate the average diameter.

Line (5) is to record the average age used to determine forest capability.

Select one or two dominant or codominant trees in each of the four plots used to determine average diameter. An increment borer is used to extract a core of wood for each tree at breast height. The annual rings are counted on each core and averaged to give the average age (see page 28).

Line (6) is to record the average height of the trees bored to determine ages.

Heights are measured with various instruments, the clinometer being popular for accuracy and low cost. Follow the instructions that come with the instrument to take measurements.

The average height is used with average age to determine forest capability. The average stand height for determining volume will normally be slightly less, by about five or 10 feet, than the average height for determining forest capability. This is to account for the intermediate and suppressed trees in the stand.

Line (7) is forest capability as read from the graph (see page 18) based on the average age and the average height of the dominant and codominant trees sampled for age. On the graph, the capability rating is class 4 for an average height of 57 feet and an average age of 47 years. This stand is capable of producing up to 70 cubic feet or just under one cord of wood per acre per year.

Line (8) is the estimate of maturity according to the following classes.

1 Clearcut
2 Regeneration
3 Immature
4 Mature
5 Overmature
6 Uneven Age

See Appendix II Guidelines to Section 9 of the Act for "immature stand."

Line (9) requires your estimate of the density or crown closure of the main stand. This is the percentage of sky blocked out by foliage when you look up. Consider yourself to be lying on the ground and give an estimate of crown closure. However, exclude the effect of shrubs and lesser vegetation. The classes are:

1 0-40% Crown closure
2 41-60% Crown closure
3 61-100% Crown closure
4 Patchy

Line (10) is for a general description of soil drainage based upon the following four possibilities. Use the number corresponding to your best assessment of the situation.

1 *Dry* — gravel deposit or steep hill.
2 *Well Drained* — knoll, hummock, hill.
3 *Imperfectly Drained* — excluding bogs and swamps, any place where there is a restriction to drainage.
4 *Poorly Drained* — bog, marsh or treed swamp.

Line (11) provides a space to rate the estimated windfirmness of the stand as follows:

1 *Below Average Windfall Risk*
   Valley bottoms, except where parallel to the direction of prevailing winds.

   All lower, and gentle middle, north and east facing slopes.

   All lower, and gentle middle, south and west facing slopes that are protected from the wind by considerably higher ground not far to windward.

2 *Above Average Windfall Risk*
   Valley bottoms parallel to the direction of prevailing winds.

   Gentle middle south and southwest slopes not protected to the windward.

   Moderate to steep middle, and all upper north and east facing slopes.

   Moderate to steep middle south and southwest facing slopes.

3 *Very High Windfall Risk*
Ridgetops.

Saddles in ridges.

Moderate to steep middle south and southwest facing slopes not protected to the windward.

All upper south and southwest facing slopes.

The risk of windfall in these situations is increased at least one category by such factors as poor drainage, shallow soils, defective roots and boles, overly dense stands, or even-aged stands of spruce and/or fir. Conversely, the risk of windfall is reduced if the stand is somewhat open-grown, composed of young, vigorous, sound trees and contains at least 20 hardwood trees per acre (50 per hectare). All hardwood stands are considered to have below average risk. All situations become very high risk if exposed to special topographic conditions, such as gaps or saddles to the windward in ridges at higher elevations. These can funnel winds into the area.

Line (12) is for species composition of the dominant and codominant trees. You can abbreviate the species by including only the first letters of each part of their names. For example, 4rS, 4bF, 2rM, yB would indicate about 40 per cent red spruce, 40 per cent balsam fir, and 20 per cent red maple and some yellow birch.

Line (13) describes the cover type. Record the number of one of the following categories:

1	Softwood	76-100% softwood
2	Mixedwood	26- 75% softwood
3	Hardwood	0- 25% softwood
4	Clearcut recently	
5	Partial-cut recently	
6	Bog	
7	Swamp	
8	Burn	
9	Barren	
10	Semi-barren	
11	Field (Specify kind)	
12	Alder	
13	Road	
14	Water	
15	Marsh	
16	Other (Specify)	

Waterfowl habitat (see Line 14).

Wetland fur-bearer — beaver (see Line 14).

Line (14) is used to assess certain features important to a wildlife habitat. The following classification should apply and more than one number should be used where warranted:

1 Nothing Specific
2 Alder Patches
3 Wolf Trees
4 Snags
5 Deer Yards
6 Nesting Site
7 Marsh Land
8 Apple Trees
9 Greenbelts
10 Erosion Prevention
11 Rabbit Habitat
12 Upland Bird Habitat

Christmas trees (see Line 15).

Rabbit habitat (see Line 14).

13 Wetland — Fur Bearing Mammals and Waterfowl

Line (15) covers the products which can be produced from the stand. List all the numbers that apply

1 Nil
2 Pulpwood
3 Sawlogs
4 Fuelwood
5 Fence Posts
6 Maple Products
7 Christmas Trees
8 Poles and Piling
9 Other (Specify)

Line (16) lists the various silvicultural or harvesting treatments which you believe should be carried out in the stand, taking into account the forest management practices best suited.

1 Nil
2 Clearcut
3 Partial or selection cut
4 Strip or patch clearcut
5 Salvage cut of unhealthy or blown down trees
6 Conversion to softwoods, hardwoods, or mixedwoods
7 Site preparation for seeding or planting
8 Planting
9 Cleaning
10 Thinning
11 Weeding
12 Christmas Tree cultivation
13 Sugar Bush
14 Other (specify)

Line (17) refers to the time at which a treatment should be carried out in that stand.

1   0-5 years from now
2   6 - 10 years from now
3   10+ years from now
4   No priority

Line (18) is to record the average stand basal area per acre (hectare) of all the species in the stand. A rapid and accurate method of obtaining basal area per acre (hectare) is point-sampling. A wedge prism, a piece of optical glass precisely ground to provide a certain basal area factor is used as follows:

The cruiser stands at a sampling point, probably one in each of the four plots used for diameter, age and height studies. Looking through the prism, he counts the number of trees in a full circle around the sampling point, the stem sections of which at breast height do not appear to be completely detached or displaced from the main stem (see illustration on page 45). Only partially displaced trees are counted. Many of the larger diameter trees will be counted while only those smaller trees close to the sampling point will be included.

Using a wedge prism with a basal area factor of 10, the total count should be from five to 20 trees for mature stands in Nova Scotia. The factor multiplied by the count of trees gives the basal area (for example, a factor of 10 × 13 trees = 130 square feet per acre). The basal areas at each point in the four 1/10 acre plots are averaged for the average basal area per acre of all species in the stand.

A separate count of the basal area of the desirable species named in the Act will give the average basal area per acre required to determine if these species make up more than 50 per cent of the volume of the stand.

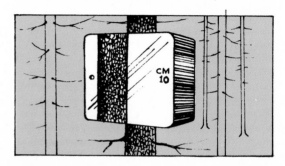

Use the wedge prism in a vertical position at right angles to the line of sight with the top edge horizontal.

The wedge prism held correctly (left). Errors result from improper positioning: tilted horizontally (centre), tilted vertically (right).

To correct for slope, tip the top edge of the prism to the same angle as the slope.

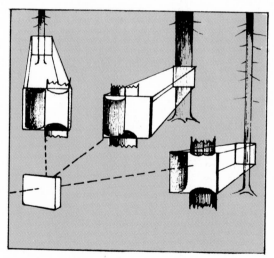

Count all trees partially displaced in the prism (centre). For borderline trees, partially displaced in the prism, count every other one (left). Do not count trees completely displaced in the prism (right).

Line (19) is to record the gross merchantable volume per acre (hectare) as obtained from the table (see page 47) using average stand basal area and average stand height. For example, if the average stand basal area is 130 square feet per acre (30 square metres per hectare) and if the average stand height is 55 feet (17 metres) the gross merchantable volume is 2,925 cubic feet per acre (205 cubic metres per hectare).

This volume is broken down into hardwood and softwood by making an ocular estimate of the percentage of volume in hardwood and applying this to the gross merchantable volume, the balance being softwood volume.

You also estimate by eye the percentage volume of hardwoods and softwoods in pulpwood and sawlogs. Generally straight, sound hardwood trees over 10 inches (25 centimetres) in diameter at breast height, and similar softwood trees over eight inches (20 centimetres), qualify for sawlogs.

The sawlogs are estimated by eye as a percentage of the gross merchantable volume, the balance being pulpwood.

Finally, record the gross merchantable volume of the desirable species named in the Act.

Line (20). The non-merchantable volume is found in the same way as in line 17; however, it refers to a volume in the stand considered inoperable or unmerchantable.

AVERAGE TREE HEIGHT ON PLOT

Trees Per Acre	2″-1′	1.1′-6′	6.1′-15′	Key to Symbols
Over 1700	A	W	O	O — over stocked
1200-1700	A	W	W	W — well stocked
800-1200	M	A	A	A — adequate
400- 800	I	M	M	M — marginal
Less than 400	I	I	I	I — inadequate

Line (21) applies to developing regeneration in all stands. Information on regeneration in recently clearcut areas is of equal importance. Make sure you visit all clearcut stands.

Under composition, you should list the dominant regeneration species with a percentage, plus a listing of the remainder. For example, 6wS, 3rS + bF, rM would be 60 per cent white spruce with 30 per cent red spruce and a scattering of balsam fir and red maple.

Under stocking, you should estimate the number per acre and distribution of young trees up to 15 feet (5 metres) in height.

The number per acre can be estimated by averaging the actual count of trees found in several (3-10) mil-acre (6.6 feet × 6.6 feet) plots and multiplying the average by 1,000.

The distribution is estimated by counting the number of mil-acre plots in which one or more healthy young trees (up to 15 feet) occur.

The above table can serve as a guide to the desirable stocking level of softwood species. About one-half the number of seedlings per acre of hardwoods are required for the same stocking levels.

Additional comments you may have concerning a stand should be written in the space provided on the back of the sheet.

AREA COMPILATION

You have already calculated the area of each stand. Now it is necessary to classify these stands by cover type — softwood, mixedwood, hardwood, and so on — in accordance with the information recorded on your assessment sheet in lines 3 and 13.

Add up the areas of all the softwood, mixedwood and hardwood stands and write the total area on the form (Appendix IV — table 1). Do the same for other classifications.

The second form is a summary of the forest land by age class (Appendix IV — table 2). Add up the areas of the softwood, mixedwood and hardwood stands in each age class according to lines 5 and 13 on your tally sheet. Now you have a good area summary of your property. It would be nice to have an equal number of acres in each age class. This would assure a sustained yield situation. However, this seldom occurs.

46

VOLUME COMPILATION

For a complete forest inventory, multiply the volume per acre (hectare) by the number of acres (hectares) in each stand or type.

Additional Reading:

BEDARD, J. R. *The Small Forest and the Tree Farm. Book I — Woodlot Management for Profit.* Fredericton, N.B.: New Brunswick Department of Agriculture and Rural Development. 1968.

DWYER, G. D. *20 Years of Forestry on Antrim Woodlot, 1951-1970.* Truro, N.S.: Nova Scotia Department of Lands and Forests. Bulletin 40, 1974. 79 pages.

FORBES, R. D. (editor) *Forestry Handbook.* New York, U.S.A.: The Ronald Press Company. 1955. 23 sections.

FORBES, R. D. *Woodlands for Profit and Pleasure.* The American Forestry Association. 1971. 169 pages.

MINCKLER, L. S. *Woodland Ecology — Environmental Forestry for the Small Owner.* Syracuse, N.Y., U.S.A.: Syracuse University Press. 1975. 229 pages.

SHIRLEY, H. L. and P. F. GRAVES. *Forest Ownership for Pleasure and Profit.* Syracuse, N.Y., U.S.A.: Syracuse University Press. 214 pages.

STEPHENS, R. R. *One Man's Forest — Pleasure and Profit from Your Own Woods.* Battleboro, Vt., U.S.A.: The Stephen-Green Press. 1974. 159 pages.

VARDAMAN, J. M. *Tree Farm Business Management.* New York, U.S.A.: The Ronald Press Company. 1965. 207 pages.

Average Stand Height (feet)

	25	30	35	40	45	50	55	60	65	70
80	600	800	1000	1200	1400	1600	1800	2000	2200	2400
90	675	900	1125	1350	1575	1800	2025	2250	2475	2700
100	750	1000	1250	1500	1750	2000	2250	2500	2750	3000
110	825	1100	1375	1650	1925	2200	2475	2750	3025	3300
120	900	1200	1500	1800	2100	2400	2700	3000	3300	3600
130	975	1300	1625	1950	2275	2600	2925	3250	3575	3900
140	1050	1400	1750	2100	2450	2800	3150	3500	3850	4200
150	1125	1500	1875	2250	2625	3000	3375	3750	4125	4500
160	1200	1600	2000	2400	2800	3200	3600	4000	4400	4800
170	1275	1700	2125	2550	2975	3400	3825	4250	4675	5100
180	1350	1800	2250	2700	3150	3600	4050	4500	4950	5400
190	1425	1900	2375	2850	3325	3800	4275	4750	5225	5700
200	1500	2000	2500	3000	3500	4000	4500	5000	5500	6000
210	1575	2100	2625	3150	3675	4200	4725	5250	5775	6300
220	1625	2200	2750	3300	3850	4400	4950	5500	6050	6600
230	1700	2300	2875	3450	4025	4600	5175	5750	6325	6900
240	1775	2400	3000	3600	4200	4800	5400	6000	6600	7200
250	1825	2500	3125	3750	4375	5000	5625	6250	6875	7500

(Left axis label: Average Stand Basal Area (sq. ft. per acre))

Gross Merchantable Volume Table — cubic feet per acre

4

Woodland Roads

One of the first priorities in placing a forest property under management is to construct roads that will bring you within easy reach of the various stands to be managed. Forest roads serve to extract merchantable wood products, allow easier access for silviculture work and fire control, and may be used for recreational purposes as well.

It is essential that forest access roads be well planned to reduce environmental disturbance to the forest. All road construction activity has a major impact on soils, drainage and the appearance of woodlands. In fact, in logging operations, road construction and skidding usually cause the greatest environmental damage.

Road layouts for blocks of land should be planned to produce the minimum road length required to efficiently develop the area. Wherever possible, roads on neighbouring properties should be incorporated, with the co-operation of the owners, into the planned network. The roads should be designed to the minimum standard required for the traffic proposed.

Forestry map showing existing woodland roads, and areas coded in the notation of the Provincial Forest Inventory (see page 82).

Woodland roads can be well planned with the use of aerial photographs.

ROAD LOCATION

Before the proposed road is marked on the ground, it should be located on aerial photographs, or a forest map using the best location based on the following considerations.

Your road system should come close to or touch upon each forest stand. This may not be possible but it should be considered.

Take advantage of favourable soil conditions so that a minimum of erosion will result. The road should be fitted to the topography and be clear of such obstacles as swamps, rock outcrops, bogs and ledges.

Roads should not be located in depressions where runoff will be concentrated. A gentle hillside location is preferable because it gives good cross drainage. It can also provide a balanced cross-section during construction, minimizing earth-moving.

It is important to avoid sidehills with slopes greater than 15 to 20 per cent and keep curves in the road gentle enough for good visibility and reasonable speeds.

Roads should be located far enough from streams and watercourses to prevent silt or logging debris from flushing into them.

Whenever possible, a belt of undisturbed vegetation should be left between a road and any body of water — streams, rivers, ponds, lakes — to allow for the percolation of road surface runoff before it reaches the water. This provides a filter to catch runoff sediments. The steeper the slope, the wider should be the belt of vegetation.

Roads should cross streams only where absolutely necessary, and then preferably at rocky or gravelly locations and at right angles to the stream. This will minimize soil disturbance and lessen the possibility of structural abutments being washed out. When construction is finished, the disturbed stream beds should be restored as nearly as possible to normal conditions.

Where possible, road grades should not exceed 10 per cent — one foot rise in 10 horizontal feet (one metre to 10 metres), except for short stretches, but then only to a maximum of 12 per cent. Naturally, terrain will influence road layout but long continuous grades should be avoided if possible.

Engineering advice on road construction is available through the Department of Lands and Forests. In addition, it will be valuable to contact the Wildlife Division of the Department during the location stage, for advice on avoiding potential beaver dam sites, deer yards, important fish spawning areas and eagle or osprey nesting sites.

The next step is to walk the entire length of the proposed road keeping in mind the environmental considerations above. Working in a downhill direction affords a better

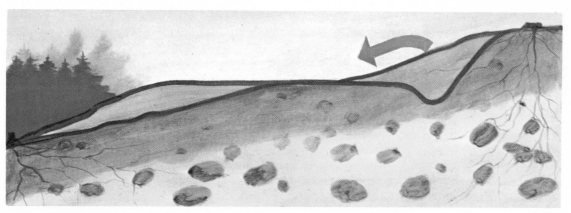

In road building on a slope, fill from the cut for the ditch (right) is used to widen and level the left side of the road.

view of the terrain. The entire course should be marked with flagging tape, tree marking paint or blazes along the centre line of the right-of-way. The marks should be made visible from the direction in which the work will progress.

Curves and switchbacks should be laid out to allow sufficient radius for trucks to turn easily. On single lane roads, turnouts should be provided to permit passing and parking. A turnout is merely a widening of the road at set intervals so vehicles can pass each other safely. Take advantage of natural passing places which require little movement of material. A minimum of four turnouts per mile is recommended. Measure your planned road by pacing the length, and indicate it in your management plan on the form provided (Appendix IV — table 5).

ROAD CONSTRUCTION

Once the location of the road has been decided and the centre line marked, the right-of-way clearing can begin. Road right-of-way clearings should be wide enough to allow road surfaces to dry quickly. Increased tree height requires wider clearing because of the long shadows cast by the trees. A good right-of-way width for an access road is about 30 feet (10 metres) and perhaps less for an extraction road.

Any saleable wood on the right-of-way and pushoffs should be cut and salvaged. On smaller roads, tops, branches and stumps can be buried beneath the road. On larger, more

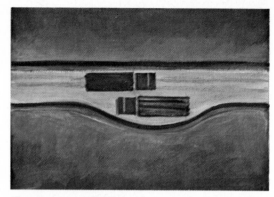

Turnout on a single lane road.

Try for road grades of 3-6 per cent.

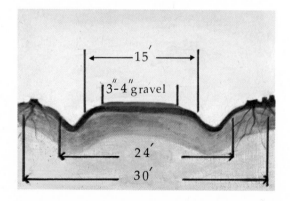

52

important roads pushoff areas should be used. Pushoff areas are sites where stumps and branches can be bulldozed off the right-of-way. Where the road passes over swampy or wet areas, it may be desirable to lay the cut trees and branches on the ground, well spread out, and cover them with fill material. The trees and branches will help support the road.

THE ROADBED

The next step is to construct the roadbed. The minimum width required for most woodlots is 12 to 15 feet (four to five metres) of travel surface. The roadbed should be as high or higher than the surrounding terrain unless the road is built through large cuts. Construction should be carried out during the season that will minimize soil erosion, preferably well after spring runoff.

Slopes of cut banks should be in a ratio of one foot rise per horizontal foot, or less. Slopes of fill banks should be in the ratio of one to one and one-half or less.

Steep slopes adjacent to roadways, having erosion potential, should be stabilized by terracing, seeding or planting as required to prevent silt from discharging into ditches.

To obtain soil material, a minimum number of "borrow pits," outside the right-of-way, should be used. Those larger than one-quarter acre (0.1 hectare) should be planted or seeded with suitable species, when they are no longer required. Fill material may not be taken from stream beds for road construction.

DITCHING AND CULVERTS

The importance of proper drainage in road construction is hard to over-emphasize. If water can be kept away from the roadbed, long-lasting roads with minimal maintenance will result.

On relatively flat terrain, ditches are usually required on both sides of the road. However, in a situation where the road is constructed across a slope, only one ditch is needed and it must be on the side of the upper slope. There should be a gradual slope in the ditch so that the water will drain away and will not seep under the road surface and soften the subgrade.

Ditches should be large enough to handle the maximum anticipated waterflow and should be constructed so that a minimum of silt discharges directly into lakes and streams.

On long slopes, culverts and runoff ditches must be provided at frequent intervals to divert the water across, and away from, the road. This will prevent the water from running long distances in the main ditches causing erosion.

The types of culverts commonly used on logging roads are log-and-plank culverts made of timber or poles, box culverts and round culverts of wood or steel. All wooden materials used for culverts should have some type of preservative treatment for longer life. Ensure the preservative is dry — it can kill fish.

Culverts must be installed at all points where natural drainage crosses a road, and along grades at intervals sufficient to prevent the buildup of water on roadways and ditches. Culverts should be of sufficient size and number to allow the water to flow without causing washouts or erosion, and to ensure that natural drainage patterns are not interrupted. All culverts should be placed at right angles to the roadbed even if this means diverting the stream so that water enters directly in line with the culvert and not at right angles to it. This will help prevent undercutting and reduce the length of culvert needed.

The culverts should be placed on a firm footing of natural material so that they will settle evenly when covered. They must not be placed too low at the discharge end because sediment may build up in them. There should be adequate slope to the culvert so that water flows through it freely. If placed too high at the entrance the water will pond and undermine the culvert; if too high at the lower end the water will create a washout pool. However, it is better to have the culvert too low than too high. The depth of fill over a culvert should be equal to the diameter of the culvert. For example, an 18-inch diameter (45 centimetres) culvert should have a covering of 18 inches (45 centimetres) of backfill.

Culverts should have a minimum of two to three per cent slope, that is 2-3 inches rise per 100 inches run, to allow adequate flow through. There should also be a rock or timber apron at both ends of the culvert to prevent erosion and undermining. This is a serious problem with many culverts.

BRIDGES

A bridge is needed if the flow of water in a stream is great enough to require a culvert larger than 48 inches (120 centimetres) in diameter.

Bridges should be constructed when the water flow in the stream to be crossed is at its lowest. Approaches to the bridge must be solid at both ends and made at right angles to the stream flow. The bridge opening should be of sufficient size not to hamper the discharge of water during periods of maximum flow. Grading the road with a slight dip before the approach to the bridge may save the structure during extreme flooding. Bridge abutments must be parallel to the stream flow, and, unless constructed on rock,

On long slopes culverts are needed at frequent intervals.

Types of wooden culverts include: log and plank (left), round wood (centre) and box culverts (right).

54

embedded about 18 inches (45 centimetres) below the stream bed. Avoid relocation of streams if at all possible and keep machine activity in water courses to a minimum.

Railway ties, 6 × 6 inches (15 × 15 centimetres) sawn lumber or rounded poles are recommended for the cribwork. The stringers and cross supports must be large enough to carry the desired load. It is wise to discuss bridge design with a forester or engineer.

Remember, before crossing a stream or river with a road, you are required to obtain a permit from the Nova Scotia Department of the Environment. When the bridge is completed, all construction debris must be removed from the site and disposed of above the high water mark.

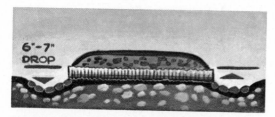

Culvert placed on a firm footing with rock apron at each end.

Culvert with rock apron and (right) an 18-inch culvert covered with 18 inches of fill.

GRAVELLING AND MAINTENANCE

Proper gravelling of the road surface provides for good drainage, longer road life and low maintenance. Access roads should have a minimum of four to six inches (10 to 15 centimetres) of gravel. The gravel should have good wearing qualities with enough binding material to compact under travel. Angular particles or stones will compact better than round or smooth ones. The road surface should be graded frequently to maintain a crown of between three and six inches (7.5 and 15 centimetres). Proper maintenance will save transport time, reduce equipment downtime, and extend the expected life of forest access roads.

Additional Reading:

MUMFORD, G. T. and S. TALBOT. *Forest Access Roads — Construction Guidelines.* Truro, N.S.: Nova Scotia Department of Lands and Forests, number 76/12/12. 1976. 54 pages.

MURRAY, J. (Committee Chairman). *Handbook for Ground Skidding and Road Building in the Kootenay Area of British Columbia.* Vancouver, B.C.: Forest Engineering Research Institute of Canada. 1976. 41 pages.

TALBOT, S. *Building Standard Woodland Roads.* Truro, N.S.: Nova Scotia Department of Lands and Forests, number 75/109/10m. 1975. 21 pages.

MATTICE, C. R. *Forest Road Erosion in Northern Ontario: A Preliminary Analysis.* Sault Ste. Marie, Ont.: Canadian Forestry Service, Information Report 0-X-254. 1977. 27 pages.

5
Harvesting Practices

In earlier days, forest cutting in Nova Scotia was of a kind that generally could be called partial cutting. It ranged from removal of a few individual trees to removal of all the larger, more valuable trees in a stand. Seedbed preparation was usually limited to the disturbance caused by logging, and was slight since most skidding was done with horses or oxen. Little concern was given regeneration, natural or artificial.

All trees are subject to normal life cycles. If free from the ordinary hazards of the forest, and left uncut, they will mature, grow old and die. Left to itself, however, the forest or stands of aging trees will eventually progress to a state where life is only barely sustained. With an outer covering of apparently healthy foliage, the overmature forest stands like a fire waiting to happen; or an insect epidemic waiting to develop. Forest animals, including the birds, are less numerous.

However, the ingredients for healthy sustained growth are all present in the mature and overmature forest; seeds, nutrients, moisture, all that is needed to produce the next generation of trees. After a proper forest harvesting operation this new life will spring up. Good forest management in overmature forests begins with the axe and a chain saw in the hands of a skilled and trained forest worker. A well-managed irregular system of partial cuts or clear cut strips will provide the diverse conditions of food and cover needed for wildlife. The forest will benefit and man will benefit from the products removed.

Harvesting practices include integrated operations (left), with cutting and skidding (foreground) of sawlogs, and the limbing and chunking of tops (background) for bunching and forwarding as pulpwood.

Skidding logs in Nova Scotia's winter woodlands with the traditional team of horses. Oxen were also used, though not so frequently today.

Forested watersheds which are left undisturbed are generally recognized as primary sources of high-quality water. Timber harvesting practices can influence water quality by causing changes in nutrient concentration, water temperature, turbidity, and sedimentation. Changes in stream water temperature affect fish by influencing their metabolic rate, hatching, development and migration patterns. Increases in water temperature decrease dissolved oxygen, and cause increases in fish diseases. Brook trout have difficulty surviving in water temperatures above 20°C.

Turbidity and sedimentation are increased where clearcutting is practiced to the edge of brooks or streams. Rainfall is not absorbed as quickly in a clearcut forest and the increased runoff has the opportunity to erode the stream banks. The crossing of streams by heavy equipment compounds the problem.

Regarding nutrient drain and the speed of revegetation, partial cutting is superior to strip cutting; and strip cutting is superior to clearcutting.

Measures to reduce the effects of logging operations on designated watercourses and adjacent to designated highways are covered in Section 12 of the Forest Improvement Act (see Appendix II), the Environmental Protection Act and other provincial and federal Acts.

58

SUSTAINED YIELD

Sustained yield is a central objective in the management of most forests. It implies continuous wood production planned to achieve, at the earliest practical time, a balance between growth and depletion, or gains and drains. Forest growth rate can be increased by appropriate silvicultural practices and thereby increase the allowable cut.

Regeneration is the renewal of the tree crop, whether naturally or artificially, and is a key point in sustained yield. If the forest did not regenerate we would not have sustained yield. The preamble to the Forest Improvement Act emphasizes the maintenance, protection and rehabilitation of the forests to provide continuous and increasing supplies of products, as well as water conservation, improved conditions for wildlife, recreation and scenic values.

Above, undesirable red maple sprouts and suckers; and an unmanaged softwood stand with decaying trees on the ground.

Left, cross-section of a red spruce cone with seeds; and a red spruce top with cones. Below, seed germination sequence; and competing seedlings.

THE ALLOWABLE CUT

The calculation of allowable annual cut for a forest property is not a simple thing. Theoretically, if one cuts only the annual allowable cut, it would be possible to continue doing this each year. However, economic conditions make it more profitable to cut heavier in a year of good marketing conditions, and refrain from cutting during periods of depressed markets. Nevertheless, a calculated allowable cut does provide a rough guide for use over a five or ten year period.

The simplest method of estimating the allowable cut is to divide the total area of forest land in all age classes by the chosen rotation. This will give a figure for the area that can be clearcut annually, and is known as regulating the annual cut by area. Taking the average volume per acre (hectare) on the more mature stands, which have priority for harvesting in the next few years, and multiplying the volume figure by the area allowable cut, gives an allowable cut by volume. This method is best suited to the forest with almost equal areas in each age class; that is, the fully regulated forest, for which one should aim.

Another simple method of estimating the allowable cut is based on cutting the annual growth. This assumes the rate of growth for softwood species is three per cent and for hardwood species two per cent. These growth rates apply to most well-drained forest lands in Nova Scotia. The allowable annual cut is, therefore, three per cent of the volume of softwood species on the property, and two per cent of the volume of hardwoods or:

SOFTWOODS Allowable Annual Cut $= 0.03 \times$ Gross Merchantable Softwood Volume

HARDWOODS Allowable Annual Cut $= 0.02 \times$ Gross Merchantable Hardwood Volume

The two added together give you a total allowable cut. There are limitations to this method, as for any method. For instance, it will overestimate the allowable cut in immature forests, and underestimate it for overmature forests. It does not allow for any increase in growth rate from improved management. If the growth rate is doubled through good forest management practices, you should be able to double the allowable cut.

Perhaps the best solution is to calculate an allowable cut as above and adjust it to the actual age class distribution in your forest. A possible rule of thumb would be to increase the allowable cut by 20 to 30 per cent for the first five years of management, if more than 50 per cent of the forested area is older than 60 years. Reduce it by this amount if more than 50 per cent is younger than 30 years.

There are many other ways of estimating the allowable cut, but they are more complicated. As pointed out, the allowable cut is only a guide to prevent seriously overcutting or undercutting. There will be many sound reasons for exceeding the calculated allowable annual cut: for instance, salvage of windfallen stands, insect or disease-killed stands, or the cutting of stands that are overmature. Similarly, there are other reasons for cutting less than the calculated allowable cut. For example, if the majority of your forests are regenerating, young or immature, probably you should not cut at all for a number of years, until some stands become mature — regardless of calculated allowable cut.

A poor forest capability, which may be caused by improper drainage, such as would be found in black spruce swamps, means slow growth and longer rotations.

Shelterwood method — before preparatory cutting (above right).

Shelterwood method — regeneration established, ready for final harvest cut (right).

THE HARVEST PLAN

The harvest plan is based on the information gathered for each stand. The oldest stands, and those with the highest basal area and the greatest volume, should be given priority in your harvest plan. The priority indicated in the field will influence your decision on which stands to cut first (see lines 5, 17, 18, and 19 on stand assessment sheet, page 39).

Obviously, stands with a considerable amount of windfall should be a top priority, as should stands infested with insects or disease that will kill a large number of trees. It may also be desirable to cut a stand of intolerant hardwoods such as poplar or white birch in order to release growth in a promising stand of softwoods which compose the understory. You may have other reasons for cutting a particular stand — concerning, for example, wildlife or recreation, or obtaining fuelwood.

In considering various stands for harvesting, you should pay attention to the various methods of harvesting possible in such stands. You should also try to keep within the annual allowable cut estimate you have made, and the regeneration methods presented in the following pages should be considered.

Shelterwood method — trees marked for preparatory cut (above right) are mainly overtopped crown classes and some codominant fir.

Shelterwood method — a seed cut five years later (right) removes intermediate and codominant trees of less desirable species.

For the table summarizing your harvest cutting plans over a five year period, see Appendix IV — table 3.

REGENERATION METHODS

Regeneration harvest methods are used to ensure the renewal of forest stands. These

methods are used to remove mature trees and replace them with new ones for the next rotation.

Section 10 of the Forest Improvement Act states: (1) A person who is carrying on a commercial forest operation shall not fell or cause to be felled trees in any stand except in accordance with practices recommended by the Board for the district in which the stand is situated; (2) the Board in prescribing or recommending cutting practices shall require that cutting be carried out in such manner as to promote the likelihood of regeneration and preserve existing young growth of desirable species of trees.

Shelterwood method — with regeneration established, five years after the seed cut the final harvest cut is made.

Regeneration is not often a problem in Nova Scotia. Cutover stands usually regenerate quite well. The difficult problem is in the kind of regeneration we get. Cutting a stand of desirable species and obtaining by regeneration a stand of less desirable or undesirable species in its place definitely degrades the stand for the next rotation. The implications for sustained yield and continuous economic development of the forest industry are obvious.

There are ways to cut trees and to manage forests in order to gain satisfactory regeneration of desirable species, and we must follow these methods if we are to maintain a sound resource base for the forest industries. Indeed, the forest economy of Nova Scotia depends upon it. Harvesting practices must follow recognized regeneration methods to accomplish the task. The careful application of suitable regeneration methods is what separates forestry from exploitation.

The three basic and conventional regeneration methods are as follows:

1 The Shelterwood Method provides for harvesting an area with one or more partial cuts and a final clearcut producing an even-aged stand for the next rotation.

2 The Clearcut Method is a single stage harvesting of all trees from an area, producing an even-aged stand for the next rotation through natural seeding or planting.

3 The Selection Method is always a partial cut, the entire stand never

being clearcut. It is limited or best suited to tolerant species. Theoretically, it provides for the continuing harvest of the oldest trees, singly or in small groups, indefinitely, thereby creating and maintaining an uneven-aged stand.

Partial cutting methods are regeneration procedures which harvest trees on an area in more than one step. From the point of view of silviculture these are acceptable harvesting practices. They are, in fact, the only options open to the manager:

1 where multiple-use considerations may preclude clear cutting such as occurs along designated rivers, lakes, and roads (see Section 12 of The Forest Improvement Act);

2 where combinations of cleared openings and high stands are needed to meet wildlife or recreation resource requirements; or

3 where clearcutting will not result in satisfactory natural regeneration of desirable species, and planting is not a satisfactory alternative.

However, windfall risk and other stand conditions may dictate that they should be clearcut. Cutting is often a compromise between desirable silvicultural practice and what is economically attractive or feasible. Partial cutting requires careful selection and/or the marking of individual trees or groups of trees to be removed, and the close supervision of logging.

THE SHELTERWOOD METHOD

In the shelterwood method, two, three or more cuttings are involved. The mature timber in an even-aged stand, or one that can be converted to even-age for the next rotation, is removed in a series of cuttings extending over a relatively short period at the end of the rotation. This encourages essentially even-aged regeneration under the partial shelter of seed trees. The trees that provide the seed should be of desirable species and form. The various stages of the shelterwood method may be described as follows:

1 A preparatory partial cut, prior to harvest, to open up the stand to encourage regeneration of desirable species. In a stand of red spruce and balsam fir, one would remove all the balsam fir and leave the spruce as a seed source to naturally regenerate the stand. This stage may be omitted if enough seedlings of desirable species occur beneath the older trees.

2 A seed cut, often leaving about one-half of the crown canopy (usually the bigger trees) to provide more seed and protection from frost, wind and sun. This step could be eliminated if satisfactory regeneration was already established, and if the residual stand was not considered windfirm enough to stand till the final harvest.

3 The final harvest cut where all the residuals are removed.

The shelterwood method is recommended for high value even-aged stands of softwoods and mixedwoods in Nova Scotia. However, there are problems in putting the method into effect. For instance, it is difficult to remove residual trees in the final cut without damaging the young regeneration. The number of cuts, timing and degree of cutting will vary with species, the rate of establishing the regeneration of desirable species, the wind-firmness of the stand and the value increment in residual trees.

STANDS SUITABLE FOR SHELTERWOOD CUTTING

Shelterwood cutting is particularly suited to the following stand conditions:

Softwood and mixedwood stands of tolerant species respond particularly well to shelterwood cutting. Pure hardwood stands do not respond as well except when more than 25 per cent of the volume is in species such as yellow birch, sugar maple, white ash and red oak.

Codominant trees should form the average or general level of the overstory canopy. Taller intermediates extend into the general canopy; shorter intermediates are below the general canopy level but do not form a second story.

The best stands should have only a small range in diameters and a small range in the crown lengths of dominants and codominants. Following the first shelterwood cut there should be few coarse-limbed trees in the stand, and the trees should be uniformly spaced rather than in clumps.

SHELTERWOOD CUTTING PRACTICES

Normally, there are three steps in the shelterwood method, but there may be two, or four or more steps, depending on how well regeneration develops, and on the windfall risk. In any case, the shelterwood method is completed over a period of no more than 10 to 20 years, depending on the rotation.

The first cut should be light, removing not more than 30 per cent of the basal area of the stand, including merchantable dead, dying or windfallen trees. This type of cutting is the first or preparatory cut of a possible three-step shelterwood. Since all overstory trees are about equally resistant to windfall, the general level of the canopy should be maintained by removing trees mostly from the codominant and lower crown classes. Emphasis should be placed on cutting the less desirable species such as balsam fir and leaving the longer lived red spruce, pine, hemlock, sugar maple and yellow birch. One should leave as many trees of desirable species as possible, and these should be well-distributed and undamaged. Trees of low quality should be removed first. Avoid creating large openings in the canopy by distributing the cut over the entire area. In stands adjacent to, or containing natural openings, one to several tree heights in width, leave the trees around the perimeter for a distance of about one tree height, until the second cut. These trees have been exposed and are usually windfirm.

In the second cut, if advance regeneration is still less than 400 trees per acre (1,000 trees per hectare) of any species five to 10 years after the first cut, another partial cut should be made in the stand. If adequate natural regeneration of desirable species is present, the stand can be clearcut. The five to 10 year period will allow the remaining trees to become more windfirm. This cut should also remove about 30 per cent of the residual basal area on an individual tree basis, with the emphasis on less desirable species. Any windfall salvaged after the first cut should be included in the computation of the basal area to be removed. The second cut is the seed cut in a three-step shelterwood. The largest and most vigorous dominant and codominant trees of good form, preferably of desirable species, should be reserved as the seed source. Avoid cutting openings in the canopy larger than one-half tree height, by distributing the cut over the entire area.

The third or last cut is the final harvest and should remove all of the remaining overstory. It should not be made until a manageable stand of regeneration, preferably of desirable species, has become established. This removal will result in a clearcut.

Where advanced regeneration of the desirable species is satisfactory under the stand to be harvested, the preparatory and seed cuts can be combined as one. In this case, the cut would be a two-step shelterwood, with about 40 per cent of the basal area being removed in the first cut. The windfirm dominant and

codominant trees of high quality desirable species are left for the final harvest cut.

The operator also has the option of removing less than 30 per cent of the basal area in any cut and making additional cuts, but these should not be made more frequently than every five to 10 years. This will spread out the cut and maintain a continuous forest cover for a longer period of time.

Clearcut method — adjacent stands of mature trees yield seed to regenerate clearcut strip.

CLEARCUT METHOD

In this method the entire stand is removed in one cutting operation, with the regeneration already established or obtained artificially or by natural seeding. The seed for natural regeneration may come from adjacent stands or from the trees being cut, if the cutting is timed to seed production. The basic objective of clearcutting is to harvest the present stand as completely as possible and secure regeneration. Clearcutting a stand with no consideration of its future regeneration and development is contrary to the objectives of the Forest Improvement Act (Section 10).

Where clearcuttings are larger than that described on page 69 and natural seeding is unlikely, or when the intention is to change a species mix of the succeeding stand, then artificial regeneration may be the most suitable method.

This method is especially useful for mature stands of less tolerant species. Natural regeneration of a clearcut area, if advance regeneration is not present, is largely dependent upon seed disseminated naturally by wind from the uncut edge of the stand, after the removal of the mature timber. Therefore, no portion of the clearcut area should be more distant from

Clearcut method — stages in a planned strip clearcut (left) with strips no wider than 200 feet.

seed-bearing trees of desirable species than the distance the seed can travel in sufficient quantities to produce satisfactory regeneration. Thus, clearcut strips are favoured.

Clearcutting becomes more of a selective cutting or highgrading operation if any number of trees are left. This can defeat some of the advantages of the clearcutting method by leaving small, poor quality, deformed or undesirable trees to spoil the next stand by their presence and their seed. These trees should be cut and left close to the ground or girdled to kill them.

Patch or strip clearcuts are quite favourable to wildlife. First, wildlife feeds on the bark, buds and twigs from the tops of felled trees. As the cut area becomes green again the light brush, including pin cherry, mountain ash and viburnums provide berries, in addition to buds, bark and twigs. These species do not hinder regeneration to any great extent. Moreover, cover is provided for the animals in the forest surrounding the patches or strips.

Clearcutting has fallen into disfavour because of excessively large clearcuts which have not adequately regenerated. Again, regeneration is the key word. If a clearcut area is large and satisfactory and desirable regeneration is achieved, then nothing is wrong. Faulty application of a regeneration method should not be blamed on the method.

STANDS SUITABLE FOR CLEARCUTTING

The clearcutting system is particularly suited to: stands with a high volume in merchantable dead, dying, diseased or windfallen trees and stands with a great deal of cull resulting from previous high grading, should be given top priority for clearcutting; the next best candidates are stands containing an abun-

Red Spruce   Black Spruce   Red Pine   White Pine   Hemlock   Yellow Birch

dance of advance regeneration, preferably of desirable species. Pure softwood stands should be mature, or overmature.

Mixedwood and hardwood stands may cause problems, depending on what you intend to grow, and on your management objectives. Poor quality hardwood stems may invade certain sites and this may be good for wildlife management but not for forestry. Good quality tolerant hardwood stands probably should not be clearcut but managed by the selection method. Thus red oak, white ash and yellow birch can be regenerated best through patch clearcutting with scarification, or through group selection cutting.

CLEARCUTTING PRACTICES

Clearcutting in stands with little or no advance regeneration should be limited to strips with a maximum width of 200 feet (60 metres) unless artificial regeneration is intended. Such strips should be bordered by forest on at least one side to a depth of at least 200 feet (60 metres) to allow seeding from the uncut border. The cutting operation should be timed to coincide with a seed year of desirable species.

Clearcutting in stands that have an abundance of advance regeneration should be carried out with care, so that as many undamaged tree seedlings or saplings of desirable species as possible remain well distributed throughout the stand, once the cutting is completed. The size and the shape of the cut may be influenced by stand conditions, wildlife considerations, natural boundaries, and appearances. In no case should a clearcut area exceed 200 acres (80 hectares).

No commercial clearcutting should be carried out on an area adjacent to a recent clearcut unless the original clearcut is well stocked with regeneration preferably of a desirable species of trees.

Where the advance regeneration becomes seriously damaged or does not develop adequately to restock the stand, seeding or planting should be undertaken using species and methods suitable to the site conditions.

Clearcutting should aim to fell all trees of all species that contain economically merchantable wood. A serious attempt should be made to market all species in a clearcutting operation, including searching out a market for fuelwood or specialty products.

SELECTION METHOD

Stands suitable for selection cutting theoretically contain trees of all ages, ranging from seedlings to mature trees. This ideal condition rarely occurs in Nova Scotia and usually only a few distinct age classes are found in any stand. Harvesting the few big and mature trees is like retiring the top executives from a corporation. Theoretically, middle management people move to the top and juniors replace them. Unfortunately, it doesn't usually work out this way, since many personnel are not suitable for promotions. It is very often the same with trees.

In the selection method individual mature trees are selected for harvesting, leaving very small scattered openings in the stand. Some trees may also be removed in small groups but the openings are still very small, usually less than one acre (0.4 hectares). Cutting is carried out at relatively short intervals of five to 10 years throughout the stand. Such periodic cutting allows for continuous regeneration, so that a permanent forest cover is maintained.

Selection cutting is often popular with the concerned public. To them, selection is the direct opposite of clearcut, therefore it must be good. However, even unscrupulous loggers have found selection harvesting attractive. What other method could be so easily interpreted to permit taking the biggest, best and most profitable trees while leaving the junk for another generation? This, in fact, is highgrading — not selection cutting.

STANDS SUITABLE FOR SELECTION CUTTING

The selection cutting of individual trees is best suited for long-lived stands of tolerant species such as beech, hemlock, red spruce and sugar maple that can reproduce and grow in considerable shade. Often it leads to the development of pure or mixed stands of beech, sugar maple, red spruce, hemlock and balsam fir. Group selection cutting will favour some species such as yellow birch, white pine, red spruce and balsam fir as well as the tolerants, but the openings have to be sufficiently large so that they approach the nature of a patch clearcut.

Land values sometimes are too high to justify fibre production alone, for example in areas near urban centres, along water frontage, some roadsides and in recreational

Selection method — the multi-storied, uneven-aged stand is suitable for selection cutting.

In selection cutting, the fir tree (above) should be cut before the spruce and pine, which have a longer life span.

and improve the wildlife habitat, quality of water and scenic values.

Cutting is not permitted within 100 feet (30 metres) of any lake, river or highway designated by the Governor in Council without permission from the Forest Practices Improvement Board. If you plan to cut near a river, lake or highway, get in touch with your local Board to learn if the site is designated as protected.

SELECTION CUTTING PRACTICES

Selection cutting practices are based on: basal area, diameter, species and tree quality. For the purposes of applying selection cutting methods, basal area may be measured at random throughout the stand with a wedge prism.

As a general rule, an attempt should be made to grow the more valuable species to the greatest diameter — cutting practices are required that promote regeneration and preserve existing young growth of desirable species of trees (see Section 10, Forest Improvement Act).

In a tolerant hardwood stand, yellow birch and sugar maple should be considered desirable species. Balsam fir might be designated as a desirable species on the Cape Breton Highlands. Red spruce, white pine and hemlock are desirable species throughout the province, but will not grow in all locations. Cat or white spruce would be considered a desirable species in certain old fields, pastures and cutovers in parts of the eastern mainland.

areas. In such locations, selection cutting may be well justified. Clearcutting definitely would reduce the value of such land.

Stands with trees well-spaced and having a good range of diameters are suited to individual tree selection cutting, providing they are windfirm.

Clearcutting should not be undertaken within 50 feet (15 metres) of a lake, stream or watercourse. Partial cutting is recommended for these borders, and logging machinery should be kept out. The result will maintain

Many stands contain large numbers of highly defective and poorly formed trees particularly after having been highgraded a number of times in the past. To improve these stands, one should select the poorest for cutting and leave the best ones.

Good growing stock should develop into valuable timber in the future. Trees left after cutting ought to be vigorous enough to grow rapidly, have a form suitable for the production of high quality wood and be free of major defects. Ideally, a residual tree should be sound, fine-limbed, full-crowned, free from crook, fork or lean, and should have a bole that is clear of limbs from one-third to one-half of its total height.

The health of the tree and its ability to grow at a rapid rate and compete successfully with its neighbour is termed vigour. For any given species, and for the same crown size, those trees with the greatest leaf area within the main crown are usually the most vigorous. Yellow-looking leaves denote poor vigour. Tight bark with shallow fissures on rough barked trees generally indicates good vigour.

Selection cutting practices apply not only to selection cutting but also to thinning in uneven-aged stands.

Consider cutting any tree not expected to live until the next cut, as well as cull and highly defective trees that will not increase in value. Crooked or leaning trees, and those with large diameter limbs, should also be considered for cutting; so should trees that interfere with the full development of crop trees.

Unmerchantable trees designated for cutting should be either cut down and left close to the ground, or girdled to kill them.

In softwood and mixedwood stands, the total basal area measured on all trees before cutting should be reduced by no more than 30 per cent. Such cutting should be carried out at five year intervals, reducing the basal area by not more than 30 per cent each time: this will help ensure the windfirmness of the residual stand.

The desirable basal area of trees to be left in a hardwood stand after cutting should not be less than 60 square feet per acre (14 square metres per hectare). Regard this as an absolute minimum.

Selection method — before the cut.

Leave as many trees of desirable species as possible, thereby maintaining a desirable stand. These trees should be well distributed throughout the stand, and be left alive and undamaged after the cutting of others in the stand is completed.

Prior to cutting, it is a good idea to mark the trees to be cut. A tree-marking paint gun may be used for this purpose. Mark the trees at breast height and on the stump, with the mark facing the direction of extraction from the forest. The mark on the stump affords a check on the operation if a subcontractor is hired to cut the trees.

Where a stand contains good quality yellow birch or white pine, use group selection cutting. Openings up to 0.2 acres (0.08 hectares) in area should be made regardless of tree diameter. These openings should be limited to one per acre (two per hectare) and be located close to the yellow birch or white pine seed trees which are not to be cut. The forest floor should be scarified after cutting to expose mineral soil. This may be done with the logging equipment or a small bulldozer, and will encourage natural seeding of the high value yellow birch and white pine species, which regenerate best under such conditions.

Selection method — after the cut.

Additional Reading:

Silvicultural Systems for the Major Forest Types of the United States. Washington, D.C., U.S.A.: United States Forest Service, Agricultural Handbook number 445. 1973. 114 pages.

HORWITZ, E.C.J. *Clearcutting — A View from the Top.* Washington, D.C., U.S.A.: Acropolis Books Limited. 1974.

LEAK, W. B., D.S. SOLORON and S. M. FILIP. *A Silvicultural Guide for Northern Hardwoods in the Northeast.* Upper Darby, Penn., U.S.A.: Northeastern Forest Experiment Station. Research Paper NE 143. 1969. 34 pages.

LEES, J. C. *Hardwood Silviculture and Management: An Interpretive Literature Review for the Canadian Maritime Provinces.* Fredericton N.B.: Maritime Forest Research Centre, Information Report M-X-93. 1978. 69 pages.

TRIMBLE, G.R., J.J. MENDEL and R. A. KENNELL. *A Procedure for Selection Marking in Hardwoods Combining Silvicultural Considerations with Economic Guidelines.* Upper Darby, Penn., U.S.A.: Northeastern Forest Experiment Station. Research Paper NE-292. 1974. 13 pages.

6

Logging for Market

Whether you do your own logging or sell stumpage you will want to know something about the different systems and equipment used. A timber logging system utilizes men and machines for the extraction of merchantable products from the forest. Basically, there are three recognized systems: (1) short-wood system, (2) tree-length system, and (3) full-tree system.

The short-wood system requires that the tree be felled, limbed, topped and bucked into predetermined lengths and left in place. The pieces are then moved from the stump to a landing by a process called forwarding.

The tree-length system involves the felling, limbing and topping at the stump. Pole lengths are then take to a landing for further processing.

When trees are felled and transported, limbs and all, to a secondary processing site, the system is referred to as full-tree.

Within these systems, a variety of methods and machines are used to fell, process, and transport harvested trees. Some people classify chipping in the woods as a fourth system.

While the sawyer cuts tops into pulpwood lengths (left), a skidder removes sawlogs (background) from the stand.

Every time a forest is harvested some nutrients are removed from the ecosystem. Clearcutting tends to deplete the soil by the removal of the nutrients with the products, and by increased runoff. In conventional logging operations on good sites, the nutrient level should return to normal during the course of the rotation or cutting cycle. On poor sites, this may not be the case and fertilization may be required to keep the site productive.

Full-tree logging, where the tops, branches and possibly even the stumps are used, may cause very serious nutrient depletion problems. There is a strong relationship between the kind of logging operation, length of rotation and nutrient capital (see diagrams, page 77). Under full-tree logging, more nutrients will be removed in the logging opera-

tion and the site may not recover its original nutrient level within a conventional rotation period. This could lead to the need for expensive fertilizing to prevent severely degrading the stand.

Which logging system is best? The choice will depend upon many factors, including the experience of the logger, conditions under which he must operate, the markets he is supplying and availability of capital and labour. More specific factors are: regeneration harvesting method used; tree species, size and number of merchantable stems to be cut per acre; the stand acreage and average distance between stands; terrain, soils and climatic conditions; and road and landing requirements as dictated by location, topography and environmental constraints.

NUTRIENT LEVELS

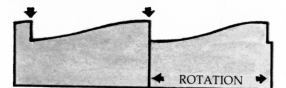

CONVENTIONAL LOGGING

ROTATION

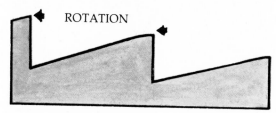

FULL-TREE LOGGING

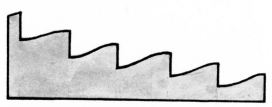

SHORT ROTATION

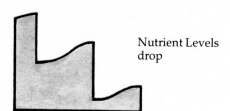

Nutrient Levels
drop

SHORT ROTATION WITH
FULL TREE LOGGING

SAFETY EQUIPMENT FOR CHAIN SAW OPERATORS

HARD HAT

EYE SCREEN

EAR PROTECTORS

SAFETY GLOVES
leather gloves
with nylon
backing in
left-hand glove

PANTS
reinforced with
nylon pads

STEEL-TOED
BOOTS
with grip soles

Left, depletion of soil nutrient capital in relation to rotation and logging system — diagrammatic.

77

FELLING

There are two general methods used to fell trees. These are the hand held chain saw and the mechanical tree shear.

Chain saw Should be equipped with a chain brake and a safety chain to reduce injuries due to kick backs. Anti-vibration handles and mufflers acceptable to CSA standards are also recommended.

Felling lever A useful tool for directional felling, it can also be used as a peavey for prying loose any logs that become jammed during winching.

Axe The axe is a useful tool in many situations and should be carried on the tractor or skidder at all times.

Many logging accidents occur through improper practices during felling and limbing operations. To protect himself from injury by a chain saw the operator should use proper safety equipment (see illustration, page 77). It is desirable to carry a first-aid kit, and ear protectors should be worn. All people working on an operation should be familiar with the provincial safety code. Beware of the common dangers in felling trees.

Chain saw

Felling lever

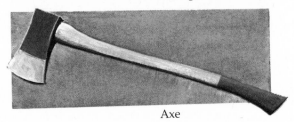

Axe

Hydraulically-operated tree shear.

Four-wheel drive articulated forwarder with loader.

The second method commonly used for felling employs the shear. The shear is mounted on crawler tractors or skidders, or is a self-contained boom-mounted unit, complete with power supply and operator cab. Shears find greatest acceptance on high volume pulpwood jobs where large numbers of relatively small diameter trees are cut, and on operations where heavy underbrush hampers a cutter's free travel from tree to tree.

FORWARDING AND SKIDDING

The method used to transport wood from the stump to the primary landing area forms an additional component of each of the three logging systems. The transportation methods include forwarding, in which the wood is carried clear of the ground, and skidding, in

which it is dragged along the ground. Forwarding is used in the short-wood system, and skidding for tree-length and full-tree systems. Roll bars or safety cabs are recommended for all vehicles working in the woods.

Productivity will vary depending upon many factors. Some of the factors may be controlled while others cannot. In summary these factors are:

Controllable
1   Load size
2   Skid or forward distance
3   Silvicultural harvesting method
4   Crew organization
5   Basis for paying men
6   Machine size
7   How stand is marked for cutting in partial cuts

Farm tractor with a logging winch.

Four-wheel drive articulated skidder.

Uncontrollable

1 Terrain
2 Topography
3 Stand density
4 Tree size
5 Tree branching
6 Cutting regulations and restrictions
7 Weather conditions

FORWARDING

The short-wood method of forwarding is popular with producers of pulpwood. The method is simple to organize and operate. A variety of machines can be used to load and forward wood. Sawlogs are also transported on forwarders with oversized hoppers. Because the log is carried, rather than skidded, forwarding will generally cause less damage to residual trees.

After a tree is felled, limbed and cut to length, the bolts are placed in groups of three to 10 pieces. This is called bunching and makes forwarding easier.

Forwarding may do less environmental damage if the cutting crew fells, bucks and piles the wood to one side on a proposed forwarder route. The forwarder drives over the branches and tops to pick up the wood and crushes down the slash without rutting the ground.

The specially designed, 4-wheel drive, articulated forwarder is equipped with power steering, rubber tires, a hydraulic loader and a rear hopper.

A common farm tractor and trailer or power trailer is also used to forward wood. This method usually appeals to the small landowner or small part-time operator because of the low initial investment. This forwarding unit is generally used under favourable

A multi-function processor limbing, chunking and stacking pulpwood for forwarding by truck.

forwarding conditions and is hampered by mud, snow, rocky and steep terrain.

A small crawler tractor equipped with a rubber tired cart performs well but is hampered by heavy underbrush, slash, rocky and swampy soils, and deep snow. It can also be used to build roads, prepare landings and perform miscellaneous functions.

SKIDDING

A popular and versatile method of transporting wood from the stump area is tree-length skidding with a rubber-tired skidder. Tree-length skidding may be used for either pulpwood or sawlogs and under a variety of terrain and weather conditions. However, care must be exercised when skidding in steep country to avoid accidents and undue damage to the environment and regeneration.

The small crawler tractor is a versatile tool for many contractors. It offers good stability on steep slopes and has an ability to work on slick surfaces. At work speed a crawler-tractor can often develop up to one and one-half times the traction and drawbar pull of a wheeled machine weighing the same. However, they are only economical on shorter skidding distances. They require less room to manoeuvre than wheeled skidders.

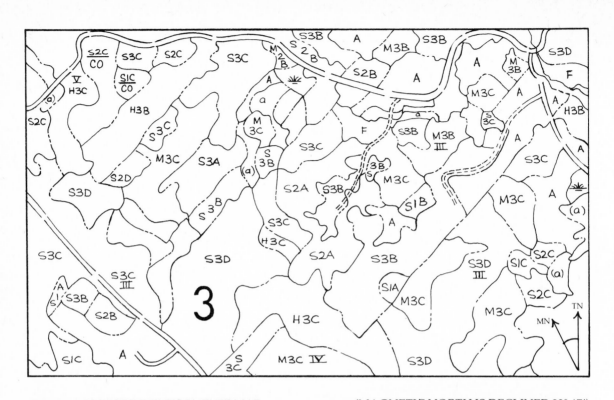

TYPICAL FOREST INVENTORY TYPE MAP   (MAGNETIC NORTH IS DECLINED 22° 47′)

Skidding with farm tractors is generally restricted to small operations, and farmer-loggers using the farm tractor to supplement their income. The tractor should be equipped with a small logging winch, and half-tracks will improve its flotation on soft soils. Since the winch is a rather inexpensive investment for a farmer already owning and using a farm tractor, it is strongly recommended for farm woodlots. Under good logging conditions, the productivity of farm tractors probably falls somewhere between animal skidders and crawler tractors. The use of horses and oxen for skidding is gradually disappearing. However, on the appropriate operations they can still be the lowest cost skidders available.

For the small woodland owner, skidding with a winch-equipped farm tractor, small crawler or animals will do the best job of preserving young growth and regeneration.

MULTI-FUNCTION PROCESSORS

Multi-function processors are machines that perform more than one function, such as fell, limb, bunch and transport. Most machines are designed for clearcutting. A few have been developed to thin plantations and pole-size stands.

It is doubtful if present day timber harvesting methods will change much in the near

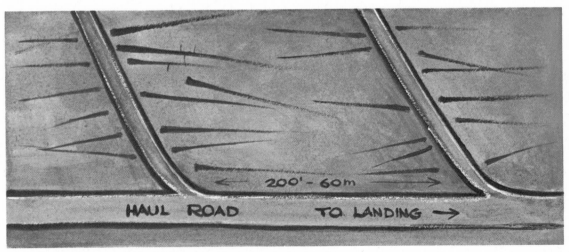

To facilitate skidding, trails should be at a suitable angle to the haul road.

future. Silvicultural harvesting methods involving partial cutting do not lend themselves to total mechanization. As paper mills accept a greater percentage of bark, chipping in the woods may make possible increased mechanization of pulpwood harvesting operations.

Light, periodical partial cuts may seem more expensive to carry out than commercial clearcutting, but they do much more for the forest. Modern technology has created some large and sophisticated machinery for harvesting forests. Many machines are so big and expensive that clearcutting seems to be the only way to use them profitably. Costs have risen, however, and their economy is now questionable.

LOGGING PRACTICES

And what about good forest management? Does the use of heavy machinery affect regeneration? Much advance regeneration may be destroyed by logging with heavy machinery.

There are good indications that a small crew working with horses or oxen, or with a small logging winch on a farm tractor, can produce a very good annual revenue from a medium sized piece of forest land. The small size of the animals or use of the winch allow one to carry out partial cuts which practically guarantee satisfactory regeneration. Big may be beautiful to some people, but small is probably better when good forestry practice is concerned.

Trees should be felled away from lakes, waterways, roads and boundary lines. In most cases, partial cutting methods are desirable.

If you must use heavy machinery, time the cutting with a good seed year of a desirable species, then the regeneration that results should be better than if the stand was clearcut in a poor seed year.

No matter how good your forest management plan is, the man with the chain saw and the man driving the skidder or forwarder will determine how well it is carried out. Only the logger can make good forest practices happen. A good logger must be skillful, highly trained, experienced and knowledgeable.

No matter what kind of equipment is used for harvesting forest stands, there are a few important considerations that should be noted to help the landowner and the logger do a better job. These practices will aid in producing better wood products and avoiding damage to residual trees and the environment.

PLANNING LOGGING OPERATIONS

Before beginning the operation, a logging plan should be drawn up. Use the forest stand map from your management plan. Indicate on it the location of hills, ravines and other topographic features (see illustration, page 82). In planning cutting operations, try to avoid deer yards and other significant wildlife habitats.

In planning the operation, soil conditions and the choice of season should be consi-

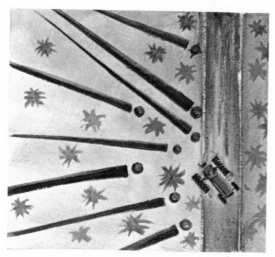

Fell trees in a direction that makes for easy skidding by the butt ends.

The felling lever provides control over the direction in which the tree will fall.

85

dered. Some soils will become severely rutted and eroded if logged in a wet season. Skid trails and landings should always be located to minimize soil disturbance and erosion.

The next step is to plan the extraction roads, the skidding trails and the location of the landings. The landings should be marked out by using flagging tape or paint. Skid trails should be only large enough to accommodate the tractor or skidder. To facilitate skidding, the trails should be at a suitable angle to the haul road (see illustration, page 83).

Where streams must be forded by skidding equipment, the operator should try to locate a gravelly or stony location. Stream crossings should be as far apart as possible and must not prevent the normal movement of fish in the watercourse. A watercourse should never be used as a skidding trail, and logging machinery should only cross at right angles. Logging machinery should not pass through immature stands or plantations except by roadways.

THE LOGGING OPERATION

The operation should start by felling the trees on the skidding trails. Plan the felling so that some trees may be dropped into existing openings and avoid undue damage to good growing trees and to advance regeneration. Not all damage can be avoided but some care will greatly reduce injury to good trees and will pay off in better future growth. Improper felling can also result in costly delays. The use of a felling lever is recommended since it helps fell the tree in the direction you want.

86

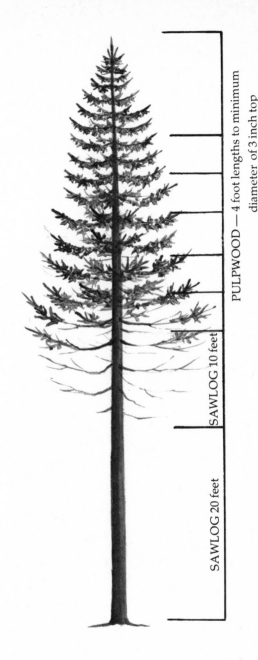

PULPWOOD — 4 foot lengths to minimum diameter of 3 inch top

SAWLOG 10 feet

SAWLOG 20 feet

Trees should be felled away from lakes, watercourses, roads and boundary lines. Any logging debris falling into or entering a lake, watercourse or roadside ditch should be removed to reduce the organic buildup in the water and not obstruct the flow.

It is illegal to fell trees that serve as property boundary line markers, and those defining cutting operations should not be felled. Avoid skidding injury to residual trees and to advance regeneration. To avoid winching difficulties, and possible damage to residual trees, felled trees should not cross one another, nor be felled at right angles to the skidding direction.

Drop trees so they will not break or split open. A big rock, log or uneven place can easily break a falling tree. Buck up trees to give the best grade of logs. A shorter log free of defects usually has a higher unit value than a longer one with defects included. Better grade logs yield more high-quality lumber and are worth more. Cut logs to standard lengths with a 3-inch (8-centimetre) trim allowance.

Avoid sharp turns on skid trails to minimize damage to residual trees. Trails should be a bit wider at the turns. On the skid trail, stumps should be cut squarely at ground level. Sharp-angled stumps are likely to puncture tires and make travel more difficult.

Logging debris, branches and tops contain considerable nutrients of value to the future crop of trees, and should be left at the cutting site and trimmed to lie as close to the ground as practical.

Before any operation is completed, all garbage, refuse, empty containers and waste oil should be removed from the site to a municipal dump, or buried in the ground where it will not cause water pollution. Fueling and maintenance areas for heavy machinery should be kept clean and hazard free to prevent pollution and fire.

A forested border of about 50 feet (15 metres) or more around all lakes and on each side of all watercourses is desirable for the benefit of wildlife. Fish spawn in these headwater streams and good spawning grounds require some shading. Erosion and sedimentation must be kept to a minimum, otherwise the spawning area will be destroyed. Cutting in these borders should be partial cutting. If adjacent areas are clearcut, trees in these borders will provide a source of seed. Winch cables, not logging machines, should be pulled into the border to extract felled trees. Horses or oxen can also be used for this purpose. The intention is to keep ground disturbance to a minimum. It is

Stumps should be no higher than 10 inches above the ground.

recommended that the width of the border be increased for every increase in slope exceeding 10 per cent.

Awareness of the above problems and the damage that can result will cause you to be more careful of your valuable resource.

GOOD UTILIZATION PRACTICES

Section 11 of the Forest Improvement Act states that:

1   "The person conducting any commercial forest operation shall use every effort to harvest all possible saleable wood of commercial value contained in tops, stumps, fir and other like species and diseased wood.

2   "When in the opinion of the Board for the district in which an operation was carried on the person conducting the operation has not complied with sub-section (1) and a market exists for the wood that was not harvested that will afford sufficient remuneration to cover the normal cost of harvesting and transportation by reasonably efficient methods appropriate to the size and nature of the operation and the location of the market, the Board may require the operator within a reasonable time to be prescribed by the Board to harvest wood that was not harvested in the original operation and that is specified in the order of the Board."

It may be an offence under the Act to leave behind economically merchantable wood in a commercial forest operation. The following guidelines have been drawn up to better define good utilization standards. Briefly, these are that: remaining stumps should be no higher than 10 inches (25 centimetres) above the ground; preference be given to the harvest of dying, dead or blown down stands of merchantable trees; merchantable parts of felled trees in tops and stumps that can be economically harvested and marketed should be utilized; and finally, no merchantable wood should be left to rot in the forest or along roadsides after logging operation is finished (see Appendix II — Section 11).

MARKETING WOODLAND PRODUCTS

The first question to be settled is: should you sell forest products at the mill, at the roadside, or as standing trees?

Stumpage is the value of the trees as they stand uncut in the forest. It is the price that a logging contractor will pay for the right to come in with his equipment, cut your trees and market them himself. In a stumpage sale the landowner should supervise the operation. The contractor may employ the landowner in some aspect of the operation. However, before the stumpage sale the landowner needs to know exactly what he is selling: the quantity of various products such as pulpwood and sawlogs, and their values. The landowner may need the services of a

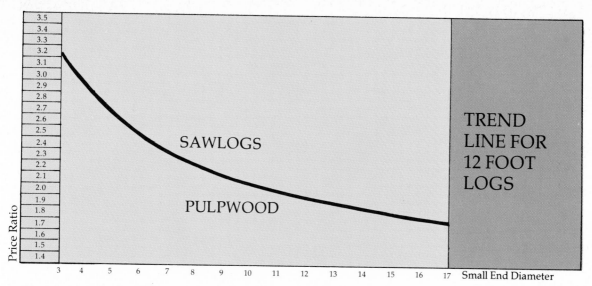

Graph to determine the minimum small-end diameter for sawlogs.

forester, and should have a contract for the sale of the wood (see Appendix V).

Subsection (4) of Section 11 of the Act goes on to say that: "The Board in carrying out its duties shall give appropriate weight to the principle that all trees cut will be used as far as reasonably practicable for the purpose which will best contribute to the sustained development of the economy of the Province."

It would be to the advantage of the landowner or operator to cut the highest value products from the trees harvested, if a market exists for them. For example, it would seldom be to his advantage to cut the finest yellow birch sawlogs into firewood. It would

also be an economic error to buck large diameter spruce trees into pulpwood. As a rule of thumb, to help you decide the minimum small end diameter of logs that should be put into sawlogs, a graph has been devised (see above).

This graph assumes that there is no change in price per thousand board feet paid by a mill with a corresponding change in small-end diameter. It is based on the New Brunswick Log Rule for a 12 foot log, with an assumed taper of two inches, and a factor of 80 cubic feet to a cord. It also assumes a good market for both sawlogs and pulpwood. The prices don't mean anything, if the mill is not buying when you want to sell your wood. Also, if you only have a few sawlogs and your wood is not of sawlog quality the method will not apply.

In order to use the graph you must first divide the price per thousand board feet that the sawmill will pay for sawlogs by the price per cord that the pulpmill will pay for pulpwood, at the roadside in both cases.

$$\frac{\text{price per thousand board feet}}{\text{price per cord}} = \text{price ratio}$$

Next, enter the price ratio on the vertical axis and the small end diameter on the horizontal axis. If the point of intersection is above the graph trend line, logs should be directed to the sawmill. If the point is below, a pulpmill is a more suitable destination.

If the landowner decides to sell stumpage, and the contractor pays him on the basis of the mill scale after the wood is cut, he can maximize his return by telling the contractor the minimum small end diameter for sawlogs according to the graph (see page 89). Of course, the contractor can also use the graph to calculate his best return from your stumpage sale. He may wish to subtract the stumpage price and the hauling cost to estimate his best return from the two products.

Stumpage may represent either a small or large portion of the value of the rough product delivered to the mill as shown in the diagram (see pages 90, 91). For example, if an owner sells standing saw timber trees, his return will only be 25 to 40 per cent of the selling price at the mill. For high value veneer logs, however, most of the value is stumpage. Generally, the higher valued stumpage can be more readily sold standing in the woods. Veneer log specifications are more exacting and logs can be more easily damaged by inexperienced crews.

Type	Return for Stumpage	Return for Felling and Bucking	Return for Skidding
Sawlogs	25-40%		
Pulpwood	4-10%		
Veneer Logs	60-70%		

Felling, bucking, skidding, and hauling are operations where a woodland owner can earn money. If he hires the labour to log, he may still receive a return for his own management. In this case his total return can be greater than a straight stumpage sale.

Although experienced cruisers are good judges of timber quality, many defects in trees cannot be seen until the tree is cut. Buyers usually allow for these unseen defects. Because there will be less defect in stands that have been subjected to good forest practice, the deduction should be less.

Although returns can be increased by harvesting your own timber, there are certain other things to consider. You will need equipment, some ability in logging, at least one helper, and will also need to plan your schedule to have time for woods work.

An alternative is to sell products at the roadside. Selling logs at roadside requires only felling, bucking, and skidding equipment. Buyers will often take cut products, handy for loading, in quantities they would not buy as stumpage. Selling at the roadside will return to the owner all profits except those associated with hauling and the final selling.

Before you cut wood or sell standing trees, you will want to know the products being bought in the vicinity, their specifications and prices. Specifications will tell you the lengths and diameters wanted, minimum sizes, amount of rot or cull acceptable and so on. Products will be broken down into various grades by size and defects. Each mill will have its own log specifications and grades.

Information you need from wood buyers:

(a) Price — roadside or delivered
(b) Species wanted
(c) Acceptable sizes
    — minimum small end diameters
    — minimum and maximum lengths
(d) Quality acceptable
(e) Permissible defects.

Type	Return for Loading and Hauling	Return for Business Profits	Value for Product at Mill
Sawlogs			
Pulpwood			100%
Veneer Logs			100%
			100%

Your woodland is capable of producing many different wood products as follows: veneer logs, sawlogs, poles, piling, mine timbers, bridge materials, fence posts, culvert stock, spoolwood, pulpwood, railway ties, lathwood, fuelwood, Christmas trees and boughs.

EARNINGS

The total return from your woodland depends upon whether you merely sell stumpage, or choose to do the cutting, skidding, and hauling to the mill. Woods work provides the opportunity to pay yourself wages for your labour. If selling stumpage grosses $350, cutting, skidding and selling at roadside might increase the figure to $1,000; and by adding the hauling and selling at millyard it could go to $1,260. Actually, a great deal depends upon the quality of the logs. Poor logs cost as much to cut, skid and haul as good logs. For the highest quality veneer logs, the stumpage value may be as high as 70 per cent of the delivered value. For some low-quality but operable stands, the stumpage value may be close to zero.

Your woodland may also be considered as a capital investment, yielding a periodic interest return in the form of new growth. The per acre return, especially where stumpage is sold, will be lower than the per acre return from farm crops, but the money invested is also much lower.

MEASURING FOREST PRODUCTS

The various products cut from the forest are measured and sold in different forms:

Firewood is usually sold by the cord.

Poles, piling and mine timbers are measured by the running foot of length, and by the piece.

Fence posts, ties and small poles are sold by the piece or unit.

Pulpwood is generally sold by the standard cord, or cubic metre (stacked).

Sawlogs are sold by board foot measure or cubic metre.

A standard cord is a stack of wood 4 feet by 4 feet by 8 feet or an equivalent measure containing 128 cubic feet.

A board foot is a square foot of lumber one inch thick, or the equivalent volume of 144 cubic inches.

A cubic metre stacked is one metre long, one metre wide and one metre high.

Standard cord of rough stacked pulpwood compared with a stacked cubic metre.

HOW TO SCALE PULPWOOD

A standard cord of rough softwood pulpwood contains about 80 cubic feet of solid wood, the remainder of the stack being air space and bark.

A standard cord of peeled softwood pulpwood contains about 90 cubic feet of solid wood, the remainder of the stack being air space.

The actual solid wood volume in a cord varies widely.

How to measure a long even pile:

(a) Take a height measurement at centres of four foot intervals (on both sides of the pile for eight foot wood). For example, height readings:

   1st: 4.3 feet   4th: 4.9 feet
   2nd: 4.6 feet   5th: 4.5 feet
   3rd: 5.1 feet

$$\text{Average height} = \frac{23.4}{5} = 4.7 \text{ feet}$$

(b) Measure the length of the pile in feet to nearest $1/10$ foot: 20.0 feet

(c) Using formula:

$$\frac{\text{length of pile (feet)} \times \text{height (feet)} \times \text{length of wood (feet)}}{128 \text{ cubic feet}}$$

= volume in standard cords

$$\text{or } \frac{20.0' \times 4.7' \times 4.0'}{128} = \frac{20.0 \times 4.7}{32}$$

$$= \frac{23.5}{8} = 2.94 \text{ standard cords}$$

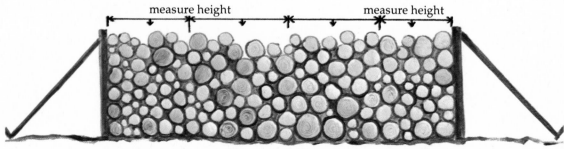

Determining the average height of a long even pile of pulpwood. Measure heights at arrows ▼

Well-piled wood is easier to scale. Place good skids under the pile on a reasonably flat surface. The pile should be straight on the sides and level on top.

Deductions are made from the gross scale of the pile for the following:

    (a) Voids or holes in the pile.

          Example: Space equivalent to a 5-inch bolt: from cull table for rough pulpwood deduct $1/100$ of a cord from gross scale for each void or hole equivalent to a 5-inch bolt. (see table on page 95).

    (b) Undersize wood may be subject to a penalty scale.

    (c) Defective or rotten bolts.

    (a) Measure the size of the defect and deduct from gross scale. Example: size of defect 10 inches from table for a 10-inch defect, deduct .03 of a cord from the gross scale.

    (b) Culls: if volume of defect exceeds $1/2$ the volume of the bolt, usually the entire piece is deducted from the gross scale.

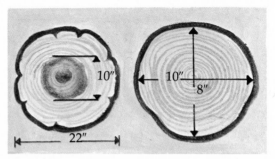

Measuring a defect for deduction from the gross scale.

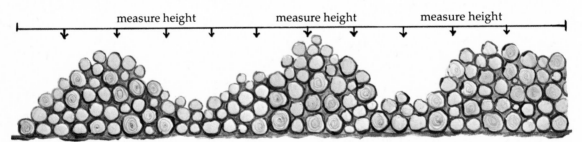

The more uneven the pile, the more measurements are required to obtain the average height. Wood to be scaled should never be piled in this manner.

Diameter of bolt or defect in inches	No. of Pieces — Contents in stacked cords of 128 cubic feet									
	1.	2.	3.	4.	5.	6.	7.	8.	9.	10.
2.	.00	.00	.00	.00	.00	.01	.01	.01	.01	.01
3.	.00	.00	.01	.01	.01	.01	.01	.02	.02	.02
4.	.00	.01	.01	.02	.02	.02	.03	.03	.04	.04
5.	.01	.01	.02	.02	.03	.04	.04	.05	.05	.06
6.	.01	.02	.03	.04	.05	.05	.06	.07	.08	.09
7.	.01	.02	.04	.05	.06	.07	.08	.10	.11	.12
8.	.02	.03	.05	.06	.08	.10	.11	.13	.14	.16
9.	.02	.04	.06	.08	.11	.13	.15	.17	.19	.21
10.	.03	.05	.08	.10	.13	.16	.18	.21	.23	.26
11.	.03	.06	.09	.12	.16	.19	.22	.25	.28	.31
12.	.04	.07	.11	.15	.19	.22	.26	.30	.33	.37
13.	.04	.09	.13	.17	.22	.26	.30	.34	.39	.43
14.	.05	.10	.15	.20	.25	.30	.35	.40	.45	.50
15.	.06	.12	.17	.23	.29	.35	.41	.46	.52	.58
16.	.06	.13	.20	.26	.34	.39	.46	.52	.59	.65

Applies only to stacked 4-foot rough pulpwood

HOW TO SCALE SAWLOGS

Measuring the board foot content of a log is not difficult:

(a) Measure the diameter of the log, inside the bark at the small end, to the lowest inch. If the log is not round, measure the smaller and larger diameters, add together and divide by two, giving the average.

	Diameter	
Example:	at small end	
Log 1	6.4″	= 6 inch log
Log 2	8.9″	= 8 inch log
Log 3	10.1″	= 10 inch log

(b) Measure the length of the log to the last full foot.

(c) From the New Brunswick Log Scale Table (see page 96), determine the board feet in a log of the diameter and length you have measured.

(d) If the logs have defects, deductions should be made from the scale.

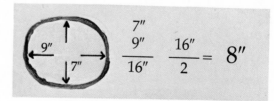

DIAMETER IN INCHES INSIDE BARK AT SMALL END OF LOG

	8	9	10	11	12	13	14	15	16	17	18	19	20	21	22	23
3	3	3	3	3	4	4	5	5	6							
4	4	5	5	6	7	7	8	9	9			Logs longer than those for which values are given to be scaled in two or more lengths.				
5	6	7	8	9	10	11	12	13	14	15	16					
6	10	11	12	14	15	17	18	19	20	22	23					
7	15	17	19	21	23	25	27	29	31	33	35					
8	20	23	25	28	30	33	35	38	40	43	45	48	50	53	55	58
9	24	27	30	33	36	39	42	45	48	51	54	57	60	63	66	69
10	32	36	40	44	48	52	56	60	64	68	72	76	80	84	88	92
11	40	45	50	55	60	65	70	75	80	85	90	95	100	105	110	115
12	48	54	60	66	72	78	84	90	96	102	108	114	120	126	132	138
13	56	63	70	77	84	91	98	105	112	119	126	133	140	147	154	161
14	65	74	82	90	98	106	114	122	130	139	147	155	163	171	179	188
15	75	84	93	102	112	121	131	140	150	159	168	177	187	196	205	214
16	85	96	107	117	128	138	149	159	170	181	192	202	213	223	234	245
17	99	111	124	136	149	161	174	186	198	210	223	235	248	261	275	286
18	115	129	143	158	172	186	200	215	229	244	258	272	286	301	315	330
19	131	147	163	180	196	212	228	245	261	278	294	310	326	343	359	376
20	150	168	187	206	225	243	262	281	300	318	337	356	375	393	412	431
21	164	185	206	227	247	268	288	308	327	349	370	391	411	432	453	474
22	181	204	227	250	272	295	317	340	362	385	408	431	453	476	498	521
23	188	223	248	272	297	317	336	356	376	411	445	470	495	519	544	569
24	216	243	270	297	324	352	380	406	432	459	486	513	540	569	594	621
25	238	268	298	328	358	388	419	448	477	507	537	566	596	620	656	685
26	253	285	317	348	380	411	444	475	507	538	570	602	634	665	697	729
27	273	307	341	375	410	444	478	512	546	580	615	649	683	717	751	785
28	307	345	384	422	460	498	537	575	614	652	690	728	767	805	844	882
29	329	370	410	452	495	535	575	616	657	698	739	780	820	862	903	944
30	353	397	441	485	530	574	618	662	706	750	795	839	883	927	971	1015

Make sure the lengths of logs, pulpwood and other products are measured accurately when bucked, by using a measuring pole. It is better to take your time, than lose out on the scale because your logs are cut too long, such as 12'9". By the same token, logs should not be cut short, or they may be scaled a foot shorter than expected. Logs normally include a three-inch trimming allowance. At all times, make sure the ends are square and that branches are cut flush with the stem.

The woodlot owner should always be sure his products meet required specifications.

Additional Reading:

Handbook for Logging with Farm Tractor-mounted Winches. Forest Engineering Research Institute of Canada. Handbook Number 2. 1977. 16 pages.

Notes on Scaling and the Measurement of Forest Products. Truro, N.S.: Distributed by the Nova Scotia Department of Lands and Forests. 40 pages.

BEDARD, J. R. *The Small Forest and The Tree Farm. Book II — Logging the Small Forest for Profit.* Fredericton, N.B.: New Brunswick Department of Agriculture and Rural Development. 1968.

BELL, A. M., J. M. BROWN and W. F. HUBBARD. *Impact of Harvesting on Forest Environments and Resources.* Fredericton, N.B.: Canadian Forestry Service, Forestry Technical Report number 3. 1974. 237 pages.

PETRO, F. J. *Felling and Bucking Hardwoods — How to Improve Your Profit.* Ottawa, Ont.: Canadian Forestry Service, Publication number 1291. 1971. 140 pages.

ROTHWELL, R. L., revised by R. M. WALDRON and P. A. LOGAN. *Watershed Management Guidelines for Logging and Road Construction in Alberta.* Edmonton, Alta.: Northern Forest Research Centre. Information Report NOR-X-208. 1978. 43 pages.

SABEAN, B. *The Effects of Shade Removal on Stream Temperature in Nova Scotia.* Kentville, N.S.: Nova Scotia Department of Lands and Forests, numbers 76/118/100 And 77/135/150. 1976 and 1977.

KIMNINS, J. P. *Evaluation of the Consequences for Future Tree Productivity of the Loss of Nutrients in Whole-Tree Harvesting,* Vancouver, B.C.: University of British Columbia, 1977. 14 pages.

WOETMAN, G. F. and B. WEBBER. *The Influence of Wood Harvesting on Nutrient Statues of Two Spruce Stands.* Ottawa, Ont.: Canadian Journal of Forest Research, volume 2. 1972. 18 pages.

7

Growing the Forest

A silvicultural plan includes the whole set of procedures — cleaning, thinning and other methods of stand culture — used in growing trees for a specific purpose and replacing them at the proper time through regeneration, according to an explicit program.

The silvicultural plan involves a series of decisions such as: I intend to grow these products; here's how I am going to do it; and this is the way I hope to ensure the regeneration of new trees when I harvest the old ones.

The silvicultural plan, including the regeneration method, must be compatible with the requirements of the trees being grown. The plan and its fulfillment are what separate forestry from exploitation.

One step in drawing up your own management plan is to recommend silvicultural improvement work. Three distinctly different silvicultural techniques may be applied: cleaning, thinning and reforestation.

Cleaning is carried out in young stands that are overstocked; thinning is done in immature stands that are overstocked; and reforestation is carried out where natural regeneration fails or is inadequate. Reforestation may also be used to establish plantations on abandoned agricultural land, and may involve some form of site preparation as well as planting.

Cleaning operations are important in growing the forest. While cleaning of small growth (left) is carried out with a clearing saw, an old residual is removed (foreground) with a chain saw.

Forestry is an action program. Although forests may be developed by use of the axe and saw, they are also easily destroyed by the same tools. Whether they are developed into profitable undertakings or destroyed depends upon the knowledge and the purpose of the man with the axe and saw.

CLEANING

A cutting made in a young stand, not past the sapling stage, in order to free the best trees from undesirable competition, is called a cleaning. This means cutting unwanted species, diseased, damaged or malformed trees, and those crowding better trees, so that the remaining trees can grow faster. Unwanted species may include beech, red maple, grey birch, pin cherry, poplars and balsam fir. It is a simple but responsible task. Skills are necessary to select trees preferably of desirable species, and to maintain a good spacing between them.

For best growth young stands should not exceed 800 to 1,200 stems per acre (2,000 - 3,000 per hectare), evenly spaced. In overstocked stands, thousands of trees die from crowding, and growth may stagnate. Concentrating light and nutrients on fewer stems increases the growth rate and the merchantable wood crop. Studies indicate that trees on some cleaned areas required only four years to grow one inch (2.5 centimetres) in diameter, compared to seven years in uncleaned stands (See illustration page 103).

By cleaning young stands we are trying to avoid small trees at harvest age (see illustration page 101) a sight all too common in our forests. Cleaning is an excellent way to improve forest growth and the desired species composition. Cleaning permits favouring one species over another, for example, spruce over fir.

By increasing the growth rate through cleaning, the rotation may be shortened by 10-20 years for spruce and fir. Making the future crop trees larger, and mostly the same size, allows for less expensive harvesting. By promoting good crowns and stronger root systems, cleaning helps prevent windfall.

STANDS SUITABLE FOR CLEANING

Even-aged stands 6-15 feet (2-5 metres) tall (line 6), 12-20 years old (line 5) on good sites (line 7) with stems less than 4 feet apart are good candidates. It is considered more economical to clean stands at this size since the direct cost will be less and the calculated long term return will be higher than for younger or older stands.

Normally, it is recommended that young stands containing 40 per cent or more (line 12) white, red and jack pine, be left at least until the early thinning stage. There is some benefit to cleaning mixed stands of white pine and red oak to favour these species, but only if the white pine is shaded by the red oak and not attacked by white pine weevil.

Similarly, because open-grown hardwoods become short and limby, it is recommended that young hardwood stands be left, at least until the early pole stage, except perhaps in stands where sugar maple predominates and which are being improved for future maple sap production.

Record your plans on the sheet headed, "Five Year Silvicultural Guide" (see Appendix IV-Table 4).

LAYING OUT THE AREA FOR CLEANING

By laying out strips within the stand one will be better able to control the work and ensure that no areas will be missed. Steps to follow: First through maps and aerial photographs, and then on the ground one should make himself familiar with the area. He should locate natural and legal boundaries and all logging roads. Then, strips should be marked that are less than 200 feet (60 metres) wide.

An excellent one-man device to make and measure the boundaries of strips is an instrument that measures thread while feeding it out. The thread is tied to a tree or branch and a meter on the feeding device tells you how far you have gone.

Right: overstocked, uncleaned stand with dead and dying trees, and slow growth.

EQUIPMENT FOR CLEANING

Recommend equipment is as follows:

1 A lightweight clearing saw with harness, or a lightweight chain saw with safety brake, safety chain and anti-vibration handle.
2 Safety boots with steel toes, safety gloves, hard hat with visor, ear protectors, nylon knee pads.
3 First aid kit and fire extinguisher.
4 Fuel, chain oil, tools and spares.

The clearing saw has advantages over the chain saw for cleaning stands. There is less chance of injury, because the operator can remain erect, and is also away from the smoke and much of the noise experienced with chain saws. From the erect position it is easier to select the next tree to remain, with the minimum of hesitation and stoppage. Cutting is easier on small whippy trees.

HOW TO CLEAN

Try to keep about 800-1200 good quality stems per acre. Try to favour the most desirable species which appear to be growing well and are of good quality. Damaged and diseased trees should be the first cut. Poorly formed and weaker trees should be cut next.

Take out the large residual trees with spreading crowns and wolf-tree characteris-

Right: A clearing saw (above) is recommended in cleaning. A lightweight chain saw (centre) is better for cutting larger trees in a cleaning. Clearing saw blade and guard (below).

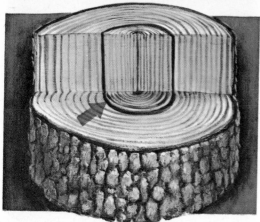

A young stand suitable for cleaning (above).
Cross-section of a tree (below) showing increased annual growth following cleaning.

tics, if merchantable. If not merchantable, girdle them, since felling may cause damage to crop trees. Notch girdling is a good practice (see illustration page 105). Leave dead hardwood and softwood residuals standing. They will fall down over the years, causing little damage to the new stand.

If there are more than 10 trees per acre (25 per hectare) of cherry and mountain ash, they should be cut; if less in number, they could be left standing. The fruits of pin cherry form part of the diet of at least 23 species of birds and normally the tree will die out before reaching a size to compete with spruce and fir.

Softwoods must be cut below all green branches; otherwise a branch is likely to turn upwards and form a tree.

Never scar the stems of future crop trees. Scars cause rot, especially in balsam fir.

Starting in one corner of the strip, the operator works into his area, cutting a narrow band along a strip boundary toward the back boundary. In this way he avoids walking in the brush and has better control over tree selection and spacing. When he gets to the back boundary he turns and starts back across the strip towards the road and so on, on down to the end. Where steep slopes are encountered the operator should always work from the bottom to the top.

Spacing should be checked regularly. Too close spacing will not give enough growth release; too open spacing, a less common occurrence, may cause heavy branching. Of course, it is not always possible to have the trees exactly the desired distance apart. (See table, page 115).

THINNING

A thinning is a cutting made in an immature stand to increase the rate of diameter growth on residual trees, to improve species composition and to increase the quality of the residual stand. Thinning may be done at 10-15 year intervals. Basically, it offers the same advantages as cleaning with the added benefit of a possible immediate return.

Thinning permits the residual trees to grow faster which, in turn, results in an earlier harvest cutting — a shorter rotation.

This produces higher value wood products in the final harvest, if the thinning removes low value species and low quality trees. A thinned stand will produce more sawlogs than an unthinned stand, and will likely create small openings for regeneration to become established.

STANDS SUITABLE FOR THINNING

Provided a cleaning has already been carried out in the stand, thinning should be put off until the trees are large enough and numerous enough to pay part or all of the cost of the operation.

In cleaning, cut poorly formed, damaged and diseased trees first.

Most stands should be at least 20 to 30 feet high. The stands with the heaviest stocking should be given top priority especially where the forest capability is high.

If the growth rings are closer together nearer the bark than indicated in the earlier life of the tree — as seen on increment borings from an immature stand — then thinning is in order.

Reserve stands or parts of stands with a high wind hazard to the last. It may be wise to consider leaving untreated strips 200 feet (60 metres) wide on slopes and ridges exposed to winds in very dense softwood and mixed-wood stands. Such strips will act as windbreaks. It may be unwise to thin a dense, pole-size pure spruce-fir stand, because of the risk of windfall.

Record your thinning plans on the sheet headed "Five Year Silviculture Guide" (Appendix IV - Table 4).

HOW TO THIN

Thinning is very similar to individual tree selection cutting because it aims at removing the poor quality, undesirable species in the stand as well as mature trees. However, in thinning one needs to identify the trees to be left in the stand as future crop trees, rather than the trees to be cut.

Wolf trees and those with spreading crowns are among the first to be cut in a cleaning (right). Large unmerchantable trees may be notch-girdled to die.

In hardwood stands, one should select up to 200 trees per acre (500 per hectare) as future crop trees. These should be of the most desirable species and the best possible quality. In softwood and mixedwood stands, the number of crop trees should be increased up to a maximum of 300 per acre (750 per hectare). The number of crop trees selected should depend on the stand conditions and species composition. In marking future crop trees in even-aged stands, one should consider marking the larger diameter trees of desirable species, if they are of high quality.

To do a proper and careful thinning job, it is recommended that future crop trees be marked with paint, at breast height and on the stump. The stump mark offers a check of the operation after thinning is completed. Blue is the usual colour marking trees to be retained in a stand. Start marking at the farthest point from a road, or at the top of a slope. Work back and forth through the stand parallel to the road, marking the crop trees on the side facing the road or bottom of the slope. Always walk close enough to your previous line to see your previous marks. In this fashion, you gradually work your way to the bottom of the slope or to the road. Take your time, consider each tree carefully. Walk

Right: Where trees are too tall for cleaning (top left), a thinning will be in order. Leaving a few cherry trees (top right) provides fruit for birds. Saw damage (lower left) invites rots in crop trees. Branches left on softwood stumps in a cleaning (lower right), may turn upwards to form trees.

To check the spacing of trees during cleaning, extend from an uncut tree a string, 16.5 feet long, as the radius of an imaginary circle of 1/200th of an acre. The number of uncut trees within the circle multiplied by 200 equals the approximate number of trees per acre. A count of six gives 1,200 per acre, with about 6 × 6-foot spacing; a count of four gives 800 per acre, about 7 × 7-foot spacing. For other spacings see table, page 115.

By working strips in the direction of the arrows, the operator has better control over cleaning and avoids walking in the brush (see page 103).

In cleaning, work from the bottom to the top of steep slopes.

around the tree and check its quality, form, health.

One method of controlling the number of crop trees marked, is to allow about 15 feet (4.5 metres) between trees in hardwood stands and about 12 feet (3.6 metres) between crop trees in softwood and mixedwood stands. A few more or less won't hurt.

Once you have marked the crop trees for the first thinning, you should not have to do it again, provided the paint stays on the trees. At each successive thinning, you mark the trees to be cut that will give more growing space to the crop trees.

SELECTING TREES TO REMOVE

Now that the future crop trees are marked so that they won't be cut, you can proceed to select and mark the trees that are to be cut in the thinning. There are three rules of thumb for spacing that are easy to apply. One is used for hardwood stands, another for mixedwood and the third for softwood stands.

In hardwood stands, with the exception of poplar, the rule of thumb is that each crop tree should have a space that is twice as long in feet as will be the desired breast height diameter in inches at the time of harvest.

In mixedwood stands, the rule of thumb is that each crop tree should have a space that is one and one-half times as long in feet as will be the desired breast height diameter in inches at the time of harvest.

In softwood and poplar stands, the rule of thumb is that each crop tree should have a space that is as long in feet as will be the desired breast height diameter in inches at the time of harvest.

These rules of thumb prevent you from reducing the basal area of the stand below about 80 square feet per acre (18 square metres per hectare) in hardwood stands and 100 square feet per acre (22 square metres per hectare) in softwood and mixedwood stands (see Appendix VII).

In selecting trees for the thinning cut, always mark the poorest quality, least desirable, lowest value trees and leave the better ones for the future. Follow the same procedure for marking future crop trees. Yellow paint is usually used to indicate trees to be cut.

If a tree should be cut which is not merchantable even for firewood, it should be axe-girdled by chopping a continuous notch all the way around the tree at a convenient height above the ground. The notch should be an inch or two into the sapwood of the tree.

Don't make the mistake of cutting every

In cleaning, spacing trees too closely (left) will not give good growth. Cutting the centre tree (right) will give better spacing.

Spacing should be checked regularly. Spacing (above) equals about six feet.

108

tree that is not a crop tree. Removing more trees than those which are seriously competing with the crop trees will harm the stand and make unnecessary work.

Many trees are neither crop trees nor competitors. Many of these will be smaller and shorter than the crop trees. Some of these can be left in the stand since they will provide replacement for crop trees that may die, blow down or be damaged by logging.

Don't thin too close to a clearcut area or open field. Leaving an unthinned strip of about 50 feet (15 metres) along the edge of the opening will help protect the inside thinned stand from windfall.

All quality thinning work requires the use of small equipment such as tractors with winches, or horses. The narrower the equipment, the better the quality of the residual stand.

THINNING IN PLANTATIONS

Basically the same procedure is used for thinning in plantations. The largest, healthiest, best-formed trees are kept as crop trees and the spacing rule of thumb is applied.

In plantations it is more economical, though less beneficial, to cut out complete

Softwood stand being marked for thinning. Yellow paint identifies trees to be cut.

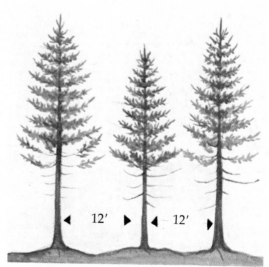

Thinning to 12-foot spacing in softwoods may yield, as a rule of thumb, 12-inch DBH trees at harvest.

109

rows rather than considering individual trees to keep, and others to cut. Usually the process involves removing every third row. This allows the use of larger mechanical equipment for cutting and moving the wood to roadside.

Thinnings should be carried out in plantations when crowding has reached the point where natural pruning has killed more than half the live branches on most of the trees. In widely spaced plantations, this may not occur until the trees are too large for row thinning. Row thinning has the advantage of making the plantation more accessible for pruning and further thinning operations. The second thinning in a plantation should not be another row thinning.

REFORESTATION

Artificial reforestation involves the planting or seeding of the most desirable species of trees compatible with a particular site condition, on lands where natural regeneration has not developed satisfactorily. Site preparation becomes a part of reforestation where grass, weeds, brush and logging slash will seriously influence the operation and survival of the planted or seeded trees.

There is a concept of forestry which advocates clearcutting followed by site preparation and planting. This concept is satisfactory if faithfully carried out by using high quality seedlings of desirable species; making sure the species suit the site and soil

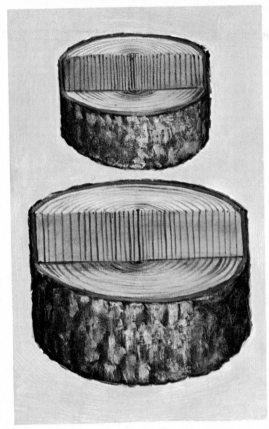

Both cross-sections are from 18-year-old trees. Proper spacing by cleaning and thinning produces greater diameter growth in the same period of time.

conditions; making sure that survival is satisfactory; weeding to make sure the planted trees don't die from competition from grass, weeds and brush; and replanting if necessary. In other words it isn't good enough to go through the motions of planting trees — there must be proper planning, preparation and follow-up.

Because of the problems in site preparation and planting on difficult forest sites, it is better to employ cutting methods that will ensure natural regeneration. However, the variable nature of forest lands in Nova Scotia precludes any single all-encompassing strategy to solve problems concerning natural regeneration.

Over and above the material rewards of planting trees, you may have the satisfaction of greening up a familiar hillside, providing cover for your favorite game, or just watching things grow as a result of your collaboration with nature.

REFORESTATION PLANNING

Before proceeding with any reforestation project, carry out a detailed study of the areas you intend to plant. This will take the form of a mini-plan to accompany your forest management plan.

Several factors determine which, if any, methods and species will work effectively and which will not. These factors include: soil

In a partial cut, crop trees should be marked to be left for further growth. Blue paint indicates a crop tree.

In a thinning, for best spacing, first remove wolf trees and dead and crooked trees, then other undesirables.

depth, soil type, stoniness (including boulders and outcrops), grass and weed density and height, brush density and height (species), slash condition, slope (topography), residual trees and stumps.

Old abandoned fields that are not reforesting naturally are suitable sites for planting. Stay away from wetlands, barrens, depressions and very heavy soils until you have specific advice from a forester. First consideration for planting should be given to areas with little or no brush or tall weeds, and reasonably level areas with few stones and no stumps. These areas can be planted more economically than brushy, stony, rough areas. Not all abandoned fields should be planted. Some can be kept as meadow areas for wildlife, if this is part of your plan.

Desirable stands that were clearcut and are not regenerating satisfactorily should be considered for artificial reforestation. Spot planting small patches may be all that is needed to provide a good distribution of regeneration. Site preparation may be required, and the operation completed within a few years after clearcutting.

There should be no need to plant partially cut wooded areas. However, scarification may be advisable to encourage natural regeneration in some of these stands.

Secondary objectives in planting the land should be decided at the outset, if uses other than timber are important to the owner. These considerations may include wildlife habitat improvement, provision for picnic or camp sites, riding trails, pleasing settings for

112

buildings, and stream bank improvement. Many of these objectives may be included as compatible with growing timber crops.

Based on the above information your mini-plan for reforestation should include the following information:

1 A map of the area to be planted.
2 Size of area to be planted.
3 Lane or access road to the plantation.
4 Layout of roads through and around the plantation if it is extensive, to make future tending and management operations easier.
5 Spacing between rows and between trees in rows.

A plantation of red spruce on a prepared site.

6 Number of trees by species to be planted on indicated areas and whether seedlings or container stock.
7 Site preparation, if any, and how and when it should be done.
8 Method of planting, by hand or machine or other.
9 Direction of rows in relation to roads.
10 Where the risk of fire is present on large areas, unplanted belts 10 to 15 feet (3 to 5 metres) wide may be left to serve as fireguards. These should be cultivated annually to expose mineral soil. The same belts can also serve as access roads.
11 Timing of inspection for survival should be noted. The percentage and distribution of mortality will determine the need for replanting. Normally, replanting should be done the second and third year after planting.
12 Weeding: plans for removing or killing unwanted scrub growth as may be required in the future.

PLANTING STOCK

Planting stock may be either bare-root or container seedlings. Seedling trees which have grown in a nursery seed bed for one year in the case of most hardwood species, and two or three years for most softwoods, are designated in the nurseryman's short-hand as 1-0, 2-0, and 3-0, respectively,

113

Transplants from the seed bed, grown in the transplant bed for an additional year or more and designated as 2-1 or 2-2, refer to 2-year seedlings with one or two years in the transplant bed.

The smaller the seedling, the more difficulty it will have competing with grass, weeds and scrub growth. Larger seedlings generally do better. Small seedlings may require site preparation prior to planting.

Seedlings germinated in containers such as paper pots or peat plugs are referred to as container stock. These seedlings are usually about six months to one year old when planted. The short time in the nursery or greenhouse, and the fact that they are planted in the field in their rooting medium, are two advantages of container grown stock. They are most suitable for well prepared sites with considerable humus, as long as the roots are in or touching mineral soil.

For a list of softwood species suitable for reforestation programs, with information on their preferred soils and other considerations, see tables on pages 118, 119.

The Department of Lands and Forests operates forest nurseries in the province and makes available tree seedlings to private

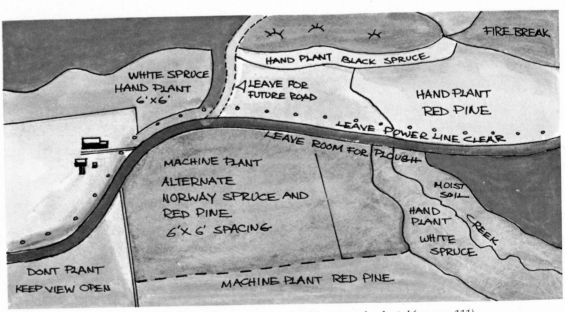

A mini-plan for reforestation is prepared following a detailed study of the areas to be planted (see page 111).

114

Rock barrens are not desirable sites for planting.

landowners who plan reforestation projects. The seedlings are sold in lots of 100 or more. Landowners should refer to the Department of Lands and Forests for further information on reforestation.

Other sources of seedlings may include the pulp and paper companies and private nurseries. Stock imported from outside the province may not be satisfactory to this climate and may have insect or disease problems — which may be imported as well.

SPACING AND PLANTING TIME

The spacing of trees in the plantation will affect their development in later years. Wider spacing postpones the first thinning and, at that time, may result in larger, more saleable products. Unfortunately, it also leads to the growth of larger branches. Closer spacing, on the other hand, will induce earlier natural pruning since the lower branches will die from lack of light; but thinning is needed earlier and the trees removed may be unmerchantable.

Number of Trees per Acre at Various Spacings

Spacing-feet	Trees per Acre
5 × 5	1742
6 × 6	1210
6 × 8	908
7 × 7	889
6 × 10	726
8 × 8	681
9 × 9	538

A general recommendation for spacing is included in the species list (see tables, pages 118, 119). A closer spacing than recommended may be advisable on steeply sloping hillsides where erosion may be a problem.

Reforestation work should be carried out at a time when it will interfere least with the survival and growth of the seedlings. Generally speaking, the spring — before the buds open — is the best time to plant bareroot seedlings. Try to plant immediately after the frost is out of the ground.

Container stock can be planted throughout the frost free period, though spring planting is recommended. The planting season for container stock can be extended because the roots are never bared to the elements, since they never leave their original medium. With proper care their growth should continue throughout the transportation and planting process.

All details concerning your reforestation plans should be recorded on Table 4 "Five Year Silviculture Guide" (Appendix IV).

The cost of reforestation will be influenced by the number of trees per acre — which is determined by spacing, accessibility, condition of the site, preparation of the site, the method of planting, size and quality of the planting stock, the availability of competent workers and proper equipment, and post-planting management including attention to tree survival, replanting and weeding. Remember, abandoned fields are cheaper than clearcuts, and machine planting is usually cheaper than hand planting.

The cost should be considered only after the requirements of assuring good survival and growth are known. There is no point in cutting costs at the expense of survival and growth. The quality of planting stock is another major consideration. Price may not be a factor here, good planting stock may sell for the same price as poor stock. The care of the nursery stock, from the time it is lifted from the nursery bed until it is planted in your plantation, is of prime importance. To plant a dried out seedling is to plant a dead tree and for every dead tree you plant the cost of those which live is increased.

PREPARING THE SITE

Site preparation is carried out to expose mineral soil, improve the site in which the individual tree is to be planted, reduce competition from vegetation and logging slash and make planting easier. Where required it should be done during the summer or fall of the year before planting.

On sites with little or no vegetation such as old fields, dry, sandy or gravelly soils, no site preparation is required. Generally speaking, site preparation increases survival and growth on soils with competing vegetation.

To survive and grow, a planted tree needs freedom from the competition of other vegetation — competition for soil nutrients and growing space in the soil, and for sunlight and growing space above the soil.

Where grass and weeds in old abandoned fields are the main problem, planting taller (older) seedlings may be a solution. If not, other measures may be necessary. The sod can be broken up or scalped mechanically by ploughing or disc harrowing. Patches of sod can be scalped with a round nosed shovel, grub hoe or spade where seedlings will be planted.

Where scrub growth problems occur on small areas, or heavy equipment cannot be used, brush and trees can be cut with a power saw, axe or lopping shears. Mechanical treatment may be possible with a heavy rotary type mower to cut off brush growth, a bulldozer blade to clear swaths of brush, or a bulldozer with scalping teeth to rip off brush and sod.

A number of mechanical systems (scarifiers) are in use for site preparation on cutover and barren areas and abandoned fields. These are designed to cope with various surface conditions, light and heavy logging slash and very heavy brush.

Chemical sprays and burning are regarded as economical tools in disposing of competing vegetation and logging slash before planting. On the other hand there are deep concerns as to the environmental impacts these tools may have. The Forest Improvement Act deals with the total forest resource, as stated in the preamble. It is not within the objective of this manual to make recommendations on these two methods.

Scarification is a form of site preparation which can be carried out in partially cut stands to improve conditions for natural regeneration. This involves breaking up the forest floor or loosening the topsoil. Tree seed of desirable species will germinate and grow more rapidly on sites with exposed mineral soils or soils where organic material (humus) is mixed with mineral soil. However, some shading from residual trees or logging slash will help conserve moisture and thereby improve seedbed conditions.

Sometimes the action of skidding equipment is enough to break up the forest floor. After winter logging, it may be necessary to return to the area with equipment to scarify the ground. Best results may occur in late summer or early fall. When scarification coincides with good seed years of desirable

Scarification with skidder using ship's anchor chains equipped with spikes.

species, adequate natural regeneration may follow. Site preparation is costly and a careful study of the need and methods is an important part of planning.

117

Bare-root seedling   *Container seedling*

TREE SPECIES	PURPOSE	WHERE TO PLANT	WHERE NOT TO PLANT	PRINCIPAL ENEMIES AND HAZARDS	REC. SPACING	REMARKS
RED SPRUCE	timber production	deep moist loams, moist soils with good aeration likes some shade	fine silts and clays		6 feet	Impt. sawlog and pulpwood species; survival in open areas difficult
BLACK SPRUCE	timber production	adaptable to many soils; peat, muck or loam	dry exposed sandy sites		6 feet	a slow growing but persistant species; frost hardy; an excellent pulpwood
NORWAY SPRUCE	timber production windbreaks wildlife	moist sandy loams; loams and clay loams; fertile sites	low, wet sites or dry sandy soils; frost pockets; poor drainage	White Pine Weevil sawfiles, spruce gall aphid; frost damage; spruce budworm	6 feet	rapid growing on the right sites
WHITE SPRUCE	timber production windbreaks	moist sands to sandy and clay loams; clays if well drained; old fields	very dry or very wet soils; in frost pockets	spruce gall aphid spruce budworm	6 feet	offer good survival and growth on a range of soil and site conditions and thus may be the safest species; grows slowly in early years; limby if open grown
JACK PINE	timber production	on hot dry well drained sandy soils	shady or heavy, wet, poorly drained soils; where red or white pine thrive	Jack pine sawfly porcupines; sleet damage	6 feet	drought-hardy

118

Red pine at 6 + years   *Red spruce at 9 + years*

TREE SPECIES	PURPOSE	WHERE TO PLANT	WHERE NOT TO PLANT	PRINCIPAL ENEMIES AND HAZARDS	REC. SPACING	REMARKS
TAMARACK LARCH	timber production	swamps, heavy clays, coarse sands, fairly moist areas	shaded areas; where water stands for long periods	Larch sawfly windfall	6 feet	rapid height growth very frost hardy plant almost anywhere
WHITE CEDAR	windbreak wildlife, poles, posts timber production	on a wide range of soils and moisture conditions	on excessively dry sites	Cedar leaf miner windfall	6 feet	slow grower, good for poor sites, valuable wildlife food & shelter, good posts
RED PINE	timber production	deep, well-drained sands or sandy loams and gravel coarse soils	shallow soils high lime soils, shady heavy, wet or poorly drained soils; older plantation refills; small openings; potassium deficient areas	white grubs European pine shoot moth, sawflies Scleroderris canker Fomes annosus	6 feet	rapid height growth produces straight stem with little taper for good pole timber, sawlogs and pulpwood
SCOTS PINE	Christmas trees erosion control	warm, well-drained soils; survives on high-limed soils & blow sands	shade, poorly drained soils; not for refilling older plantations	sawflies, shoot moth, snow breakage, mice and porcupines	6 feet	good Christmas trees if tended properly
WHITE PINE	timber production	moist soils, sandy loams or loamy soils; well drained clays; sandy clay	very dry, light sandy soils, very exposed areas	White pine weevil White pine blister rust; mice and snow damage	6 feet	fairly fast growing; consider enemies; avoid currants and gooseberry sites

Hand planting bare-root red pine seedling.

TRANSPORTING AND HANDLING

Arrange to plant trees as soon as possible after the frost is out of the ground, and as soon as practical after they are received from the nursery. In hot spells, be especially careful that trees do not dry out.

In transporting bare root stock: trees should be moved from the nursery to the planting site as quickly as possible; keep the trees well covered with a tarpaulin while in transit by open truck to avoid drying out by wind and sun; truck by night if possible; dampen the protective layer of moss or other packing medium in bales or crates; avoid crushing or breaking tops of trees exposed in bales.

During the planting operation: place the bundles of trees in pails with about two inches of water or moist moss in the bottom; keep the roots moist at all times; avoid breaking or stripping the tender bark on tree roots when untangling them from the bundle; remove only one tree at a time when ready to put it in the ground; ensure that open boxes, bales or bags of trees are protected from exposure to wind or sun while being moved around the planting site. Rough treatment and too much exposure will kill trees.

Container stock is usually transported on specially designed racks or trays — with airspace between — permitting stacking without damage to the seedlings.

In transporting and storing containers: make sure that the containers are well-ventilated; keep the containers relatively moist; keep the containers away from direct

sunlight to reduce evaporation, but not in dense shade; don't store one on top of the other for more than two or three days.

In holding the trees until planting, for one to two days: choose a cool cellar, cold storage plant, root house or a sheltered shady spot near a source of water; pile bales, crates, boxes or bags in single rows with space between packages for air circulation; moisten the moss covering the tree roots in bales, boxes or crates as necessary; seedlings packed in paper bags can be stored for a few days without moistening, but don't open the bags.

It is best not to order trees for more than two days planting at a time. If holding for more than two days is unavoidable: dig a "V" shaped trench in a moist, not wet, sheltered spot near the planting site; place the tree bundles in single file along the trench and pack moist earth firmly around the roots; do not cover the tops of the trees; water them each evening.

PLANTING METHODS

The wedge method is preferred for most open-field planting of bare root seedlings since heavy sod cover is often present. In other situations, other methods may be superior.

If planters work in pairs, one carries a spade or round shovel and prepares the hole or slit. His partner carries the pail of trees, flicks the tree roots into place with the root collar at ground level, and firms the earth around the seedling. However, eight to ten persons working individually under a crew boss, is more efficient.

During planting, keep seedlings in a pail with enough water to cover the roots, until ready to put in the ground. Do not leave roots exposed to dry out.

Seedlings may be held on the planting site for two or more days by heeling-in as follows: Dig V-trench, place seedlings, partially fill the trench with loose soil, water well, complete filling with soil, and firm well.

Spread roots and keep the root collar at ground level.

Container seedlings can be planted by any of the hand planting methods described. However, a number of special tools have been developed specifically for container planting. These include the dibble, pottiputki and corer (see illustration page 124).

In planting abandoned fields straight rows can best be made by using flags on poles. The poles should be equal in length to the space between rows. Two flags are used at each end of the field to be planted. In starting, set two flags about forty feet apart in line on the first row, and at the other end of the field opposite the starting point. The planter can determine whether or not he is on line by standing so that the two sets of flags line up. Before starting down the row, a flag should be set as a guide for the return trip from the other end of the field.

The lead man starts to plant along the first row followed by the second man who gauges his distance and direction from the first. The rest of the planting crew follow a similar pattern so that, viewing the whole crew from right to left, each man is one row to the left

The slit method of planting, using a shovel or spade.

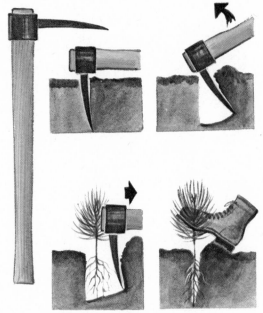

The slit method of planting, using a grub hoe.

and one tree space behind his neighbor on his right. On reaching the far end, they wheel to the left and return with the lead man lining up with the flag placed earlier and at the proper spacing from the last row planted. Spacing in the row is usually determined by pacing (see diagram page 38).

Machine planting attachments for farm tractors are especially suitable for stone free soils with no scrub growth. Heavy duty planters mounted on crawler tractors are capable of planting site-prepared cutover land and barrens. These are capable of planting both seedlings and containers. The person riding the machine regulates tree spacing in the row. The tractor operator controls the space between rows. A third member may be used to keep the trees sorted and ready for planting.

Machines may have either drag or three-point hitch attachments to the tractor. Each machine features a rolling coulter which cuts the sod, and a rigid trencher which opens up a slit or trench to receive the tree roots which are flicked into place at the proper level by the man on the machine. The rubber-tired packing wheels, astride the trench, pack the soil around the tree.

Some machines have sod scalper attachments which scrape off one to two inches (2 to 5 centimetres) depth of sod on each side of the coulter and push it to either side. The use of a scalping attachment may allow better survival in heavy sods on dry sites, but on wet sites the seedlings are planted a little deeper than is desirable, which may increase the mortality. The humps and ditches resulting from sod

123

Pottiputki — container seedlings are placed in the top of the tube. The lower end of the pottiputki is inserted in the soil, which is opened by foot-operated jaws. A hand-operated trigger at the top releases the seedling into the soil.

Corer — a tool similar to a bulb planter, cuts a plug of soil, which is thrown to one side. The container seedling is placed in the planting tube attached to the handle.

Dibble — a solid steel instrument inserted into the soil by foot-pedal. It makes a hole to receive the container seedling, which is inserted by hand.

scalping may make future plantation management more difficult.

Check the scalping, planting depth and packing regularly to ensure that the tree is held firmly in place with ample soil covering well spread roots.

Regardless of the method of planting, observe the following rules to improve survival: remove the trees one at a time from the container so no roots dry out; plant the tree so it stands erect with the root collar at ground level; be sure that the hole or trench is deep enough to avoid cramping the tree roots in order to offset root deformities; pack the soil firmly around the tree.

PLANTATION MANAGEMENT

In planting, the heaviest losses usually occur during the first two years. Where heavy losses occur, replanting should be undertaken the following spring, and in no case delayed beyond the first five years. How much replanting should be done will depend upon the owner's objectives in planting, and acceptable percentages of loss should be indicated in the planting plan.

Common practice is to assess survival in the first, second and fifth growing seasons. Early spring is the preferred season for this chore, when the trees are least obscured by snow or grass. Losses may be distributed across the area or in patches. If the general survival is too low, say 30 per cent, or there are extensive dead patches, replanting should be done the following spring.

A tree-planting machine drawn by a farm tractor.

GUIDE TO REPLANTING

(a) Check survival by a systematic survey. One method is to count five consecutive trees along a row and record them as living, dead or missing; then move to the next row and repeat the count; and so on across the contour of the land to each successive row. The percentage of survival is the number of living trees in a total count of 100.

(b) Try to determine the reasons for failure, such as: improper planting; grass and weed competition; girdling by mice; tops chewed off by animals; poor drainage; frost pockets; drought. Take steps to correct or avoid such problems when replanting.

(c) Decide if competing grass, weeds or shrubs should be reduced before planting more trees.

(d) For sawlog production, 80 per cent is an acceptable survival if there are no large gaps. Under favourable conditions of open field planting, 75 to 80 per cent is the usual objective.

(e) Replant with the original species unless valid reasons for changing prevail. For example, on a consistently dry site, a hardier, more drought-resistant species may have to be substituted.

(f) Hand planting is usually the only feasible method of replanting.

WEED AND BRUSH CONTROL

If you have done a good job of site preparation, your plantation may not need any additional work for a couple of years, and by then the planted trees may outgrow the grasses and weeds. Damage to planted trees by mice and other rodents is greatly reduced by controlling the weeds and brush around the trees.

As the planted trees are released from weeds and brush they should grow above the competition and probably will not require any additional cultural measures for a number of years. However, weeding may be required if the trees become overtopped or shaded. To weed the plantation move along the rows cutting down the volunteer growth with a brush axe. Cut only those trees that directly interfere with those planted.

PRUNING

Pruning is the removal of live or dead branches from standing trees to produce more valuable knot-free lumber or veneer than would otherwise result. Prune only vigorous crop trees and these dominants and co-dominants should then be released by thinning. It is generally recommended that spruce and fir not be pruned. Here is how to do the job properly:

Select only 200-300 crop trees per acre (500-700 per hectare) for pruning. Never prune more than one-third of the live crown of a tree.

Never use an axe. The best results are achieved with a hand saw or pruning saw. Pruning shears may work well on branches under one-half inch (one centimetre) in diameter but usually leave a short stub. Try to shear off as close to the trunk as possible.

Saw off branches using an undercut first (to prevent stripping bark from the trunk), then an upper cut. Saw as close to the trunk as possible but do not damage the trunk bark.

Pruning branches — dead or alive — close to the trunk, allows quick and complete healing.

Never use an axe in pruning. Best results are obtained with a long-handled pruning saw. Make an undercut first.

When pruning dead branches cut through the callus or scar-tissue at its base to promote rapid healing. This is best done during the winter months and before the tree exceeds 4-5 inches diameter at breast height. The maximum height for pruning is usually about 17 feet, and may be carried out in two stages.

THINNING

Although it is essential that the planted trees crowd each other while they are young, to produce good form and quality wood, there comes a time when each tree requires more growing space. This is indicated when the diameter growth of the dominant trees in the stand starts to slow down. Thinning is generally not required before a plantation is 25 to 30 years old under normal spacing (for specific considerations see Thinning, page 104).

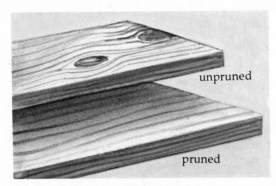

Pruning produces more knot-free, higher grade lumber.

Additional Reading:

HAWBOLDT, L.S. and G. L. SAUNDERS. *A Guide to Forest Practices*. Truro, N.S.: Nova Scotia Department of Lands and Forests. 1966. 23 pages.

SMITH, D. M. *The Practice of Silviculture*. New York, U.S.A.: John Wiley and Sons Inc. 1962. 7th edition. 525 pages.

Response to Cleaning Spruce — Fir Stands in Nova Scotia.: An Interim Assessment. 17 pages: *A 10-year Assessment*. 7 pages. Truro, N.S.: Nova Scotia Department of Lands and Forests.

BASKERVILLE, G. *Response of Young Fir and Spruce to Release from Shrub Competition*. Fredericton, N. B.: Canadian Forestry Service. Technical Note number 98. 1961. 14 pages.

ROBERTSON, R. G., J. R. BURGESS and D. L. DENT. *A Cleaning Manual for Nova Scotia Forests*. Truro, N.S.: Nova Scotia Department of Lands and Forests. 1977. 55 pages.

A Softwood Release Cut in Nova Scotia. Truro, N.S.: Nova Scotia Department of Lands and Forests. 6 pages.

PHILBROOK, J. S. *A Stocking Guide for Eastern White Pine*. Upper Darby, Penn., U.S.A.: Northeastern Forest Experiment Station. 1973. Research Note NE-168. 3 pages.

A Guide to Handling and Planting Nursery Stock. Truro, N.S.: Nova Scotia Department of Lands and Forests.

Growing Your Own Trees. Truro, N.S.: Nova Scotia Department of Lands and Forests. 19 pages.

ROBERTSON, R. G., J. R. BURGESS, J. L. PETERS and D. J. RUSSELL. *A Planting Manual for Nova Scotia*. Truro, N.S.: Nova Scotia Department of Lands and Forests. 1975.

STIELL, W. M. and A. B. BERRY. *A 20-year Trial of Red Pine Planted at Seven Spacings*. Ottawa, Ont.: Canadian Forestry Service. Forest Management Institute Information Report FRM-X-97. 1977. 25 pages.

AUDUS, L. J. *Herbicides — Volume I and II: Physiology, Biochemistry, Ecology*. New York, U.S.A.: Academic Press. 2nd edition. 1976.

FULLER, J. G. *The Poison That Fell from the Sky*. New York, U.S.A.: Berkley Publishing Corporation. 1979. 163 pages.

8

Sugarbush and Christmas Trees

Sugar maple is the preferred species for sap production. It produces the most sap and the sweetest sap. Red maples may also be tapped in sugarbushes containing a high percentage of sugar maples, but the sap is less sweet and more boiling time and more fuel are required to produce syrup.

SUGARBUSH MANAGEMENT

Stands suitable for developing into sugar-bushes are as follows: stands in which the basal area of sugar maple is equal to or greater than the basal areas indicated in the table on page 131, according to the average diameter of sugar maples in the stand. In using the table, first estimate the average stand diameter for sugar maple only, then use a wedge prism to estimate the basal area per acre of sugar maple by counting only the sugar maple "in" trees (see page 44).

In the sugar woods (left), modern tubing networks to collect sap from individual trees, are supplanting the old-fashioned sap pail.

Remember, hardwood stands are preferred over mixedwoods stands. Stands on south slopes are preferred over those on north slopes. East and west facing slopes are better than north-facing slopes but not quite as good as south-facing slopes. The stands should be sheltered by a windbreak, or other stands, from cold winds in spring.

The ideal sugar maple for sap production has a deep, wide, dense crown.

The maples in the stand must be reasonably healthy and sound. The soil must be deep enough to allow for good root development and have adequate drainage. There should be a good covering of leaf litter and good humus development.

Tubing systems with vacuum pumping will double sap yields and greatly reduce labour costs. However, such systems must be established on slightly sloping land, so that the main lines in a tubing system will all end up at one low location where the sugarhouse should be located.

STANDS FOR SYRUP PRODUCTION

Stands suitable for immediate syrup production must have all the characteristics listed above, plus at least 70 tapholes per acre (175 per hectare) in trees 10 inches (25 centimetres) and over in diameter. This can be calculated using the maple sugarbush inventory work sheet (see page 132).

Sugar Maple Average Stand Diameter		Average Crown Diameter		Sugar Maple Trees Per Acre (hectare Natural Stands		Approx. Spacing Between Trees		Taps Per Tree	Residual Basal Area After Thinning Maple Only Natural Stands	
Inches	cm	Feet	Metres	Acres	Hectares	Feet	Metres		sq. ft./acre	m²/ha
4	10	17	5	167	417	17	5	0	15	3
6	15	20	6	126	315	20	6		25	6
8	20	23	7	98	245	23	7	1	34	8
10	25	25	8	79	197	25	8		43	10
12	30	28	8	64	160	27	8		50	11
14	35	31	9	54	135	30	9	2	58	13
16	40	33	10	46	115	33	10		64	15
18	45	36	11	39	97	36	11	3	69	16
20	50	38	12	34	85	39	12		74	17
22	55	41	12	30	75	41	12	4	79	18
24	60	44	13	26	65	44	13		82	19
26	66	46	14	23	57	47	14	5	85	19
28	71	49	15	21	52	49	15		89	20
30	76	52	16	19	47	52	16		93	21

Use a wedge prism to determine the maple trees to be tallied at a number of points in the proposed sugarbush. Tally each tree by diameter group, estimating the diameters by eye. Write down each tree tallied by diameter group in column one. Now multiply the number of trees tallied in each diameter group by the tree factor and divide by the number of sampling points used. This gives you the number of trees per acre (hectare) by diameter group. Add the groups in column three and multiply the totals by the number of tapholes per tree, and this gives you the number of tapholes per acre (hectare) in each diameter group. The total at the bottom gives the number of tapholes per acre (hectare) in all diameter groups. If this figure exceeds 70 per acre (175 per hectare) you likely have a viable sugarbush.

131

Tree	DBH	(1) Maple Tally	(2) Tree Factor		(3) Trees (Divide by number of points)*		Tapholes per tree	Tapholes per	
inches	cm		English	Metric	Acre	Hectare		Acre	Hectare
10	25		18	40					
11	27		15	34					
	29			30					
				Total			× 1 =		
12	31		13	26					
13	33		11	23					
14	35		9	21					
				Total			× 2 =		
15	37		8	19					
16	40		7	16					
18	45		6	12					
				Total			× 3 =		
20	50		5	10					
22	55		4	8					
24	60		3	7					
				Total			× 4 =		
26	65		3	6					
28+	70+		2	5					
				Total			× 5 =		
B.A./Acre (hectare):									
Total									
*Number of Sampling Points: 1 2 3 4 5 6 7 8 9 10 11 12 13 14 15 (circle)									

Maple Sugarbush Inventory Work Sheet

SUGARBUSH SILVICULTURE

Begin by removing species other than sugar maple, but don't thin the stand too heavily, or to the point where it will be subject to windthrow. You may wish to keep, and tap, some red maples where there is a lack of sugar maples. When plastic tubing is used, costs increase if lines have to pass other species. Softwoods should be removed because they shade the tubing and delay the thawing of the ice in the lines.

Provide enough growing space for each selected tree to develop and maintain a large, long, dense crown. The larger the crown, the greater the sap yield, and often the sugar content is higher. A continuous program of selection thinning will increase maple syrup production from most sugarbushes.

The sweeter trees will produce more syrup with less fuel for evaporation. When there are no unwanted species in a sugarbush, and when the sugar maples require a thinning to develop better crown systems, refractometer studies in the spring or fall should provide the basis for choosing trees that should be cut. Trees having sap with a low sugar content according to the refractometer should be considered first for removal. However, size, vigour and tree spacing must also be considered.

Keep the edges of the sugar bush dense along its boundary lines, roads, power lines and other borders, for about 25 feet (7.5 metres) to help prevent wind damage.

Large, overmature trees should be harvested before they become completely deca-

This maple stand is too heavily stocked to develop large crowns suitable for maple sap production. A thinning is required.

Tubing systems for sap collection are more efficient than sap pails, but require sloping sites.

dent. Encourage the development of young sugar maples to replace those removed. Suppressed sugar maple trees are somewhat unproductive and don't respond favourably to release. Planting is usually not required, but a weeding operation to clip out unwanted species in the regeneration may be needed.

Harvesting to meet short term financial needs is not recommended for maple sugarbushes. Many residual trees may be damaged and the best trees for sawlogs may be the best sap and sugar producers. The removal of many trees may make the maple syrup operation unprofitable.

The management of a sugarbush and the sap collection and syrup production techniques are changing rapidly as research develops new economical methods. We recommend strongly that sugarbush owners contact a maple syrup specialist annually for an inspection of the operation and advice on improvements.

It is beyond the scope of this book to provide details on maple sap gathering, syrup production, and more detailed sugarbush silviculture. If you feel you have a good sugarbush according to the standards above, you should contact the Department of Lands and Forests or the Department of Agriculture and Marketing for more information and help.

Additional Reading:

Sugarbush

COONS, C. F. *Sugar Bush Management for Maple Syrup Producers.* Toronto, Ont.: Ontario Ministry of Natural Resources. 1975. 41 pages.

LANCASTER, K. F., R. S. WALTERS, F. M. LAING and R. T. FOULDS. *A Silvicultural Guide for Developing a Sugarbush.* Washington, D.C., U.S.A.: United States Department of Agriculture. Forest Service Research Paper NE-286. 1974. 11 pages.

Christmas tree stand developing on a cutover.

CHRISTMAS TREE MANAGEMENT

Christmas trees yield the highest stumpage revenue of any forest product. It takes a lot of work to grow good quality Christmas trees. Cleaning, shearing, fertilizing and control of unwanted shrub competition are time consuming operations. A commitment to this kind of work is a pre-requisite. Don't take on more area than you can adequately work. It is estimated that one man working part time can maintain 10 to 20 acres (4 - 8 hectares).

The Department of Lands and Forests employs a full time Christmas tree specialist to advise growers on all matters pertaining to Christmas tree management.

SUITABLE AREAS

The area for Christmas tree management must be reasonably accessible by road, but some control may be required to keep out tree thieves. The site is very important. Wet soils, frost pockets and hollows, and areas exposed to high winds should be avoided. The soil is the most important factor. Generally speaking the better the soil, the better the results. Deep well-drained loams are the best.

For a quicker return on investment, clearcut stands that are regenerating heavily with balsam fir are preferred over areas that must be planted. Such areas should have enough trees so that cleaning will leave from 600 to 1,200 trees per acre (1,500 to 3,000 per hectare) not over six feet (1.8 metres) in height, and well distributed over the area. Ideally, 100 trees per acre per year is a good harvest, though most growers seldom achieve this goal.

Areas with the least amount of brush and competition from other species, and a suitable amount of balsam fir, should be given priority.

Two management choices are open to the grower, the choice depending on circumstances, and particularly on the size of the Christmas tree area: (a) develop an all-sized stand of trees over the entire area; or (b) aim for blocks of even-sized stands of trees over the entire area.

Under the first option, Christmas tree silvicultural work and harvesting is spread over the whole area annually, making this the more practical choice on a small area, with the annual harvesting done by selection cutting.

In the second option, the total area is divided into blocks corresponding in number to the total number of years required to grow crop trees from seedlings or transplants, to harvestable size; that is the rotation. The objective is to have a block ready for clearcut harvest each year. This is the more practical choice for a large Christmas tree management unit.

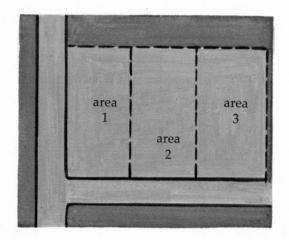

Planning and lining off the Christmas tree stand for weeding and thinning will save time and be more efficient.

136

Careful thinning provides space for each crop tree to develop fully, and can yield more of the higher quality trees.

WEEDING AND THINNING

Unmanaged natural fir stands seldom produce quality trees in any number. The first step to a profitable lot is to remove competing trees and shrubs and thin the remaining crop trees. A little organization before you begin, will make the operation more efficient. Line off the work with string or flagging tape. Sometimes you can use natural dividers such as roads or brooks for the same purpose. Mark off the areas in sequence and move from one to another until the job is finished.

With few exceptions, unweeded stands produce poor trees because crowding from hardwoods and bushes prevents proper growth and damages twigs and needles. Where there is a high percentage of weed species, you may wish to remove these first, and space or thin the remaining fir in a second step. On the other hand, if weed trees are scattered, it may be better to combine the operations.

In the management of Christmas tree stands, stumps and exposed roots of hardwoods, may tend to sprout and sucker. This can be reduced by treating freshly cut stumps with a suitable herbicide.

Weeding leaves a lot of top and limb material on the ground. Unless it interferes with young trees or poses a serious fire hazard, leave it to rot back into the soil. To hasten this process, always lop trees so the wood will lie close to the ground and thus decompose quickly.

Thinning concerns the removal of trees to allow sufficient space for each potential crop tree to develop properly. As a general rule, select the most desirable trees and thin around them. The correct distance apart will depend upon the height and condition of the stand. Only experience will allow you to produce the best results every time.

In a stand of all-sized trees, thin to give a range of sizes. In a stand of blocks of even-sized trees, thin to produce uniformly optimum sized trees.

Keep in mind that your goal is to grow marketable trees six to eight feet tall (2-3 metres), as soon as possible. These should have dense foliage, a dark green colour, and a base roughly two-thirds the height. Remember, the trees *will* grow. Leave them elbow-room. Overcrowding rapidly spoils upcoming Christmas trees.

Two common mistakes include thinning too lightly (since leaving trees too close together results in poorly formed trees that are hard to sell); and not keeping in mind the future growth of the stand (it is harder and more costly to correct defects in older trees and make a marketable product).

In any group of trees, cut the obvious one first. If you have the choice of two trees, consider the following: whorl development, bottom whorl and handle, regeneration around and under each potential crop tree, and internodal bud development. Remove barren or budless stems which cannot respond quickly to shearing.

Plan to do one operation at a time. When working alone much time will be lost if you try to thin, under prune, and treat stumps all at once. It is more efficient to lay out your strip and work with one tool at a time.

Do not thin more than you can maintain. You should aim for maximum production from each and every acre you thin and weed. The purpose of an initial thinning is only to allow the remaining trees to develop into marketable products, and this calls for annual maintenance.

Weeding and thinning are ongoing operations, required every year. After you have carefully thinned and weeded to produce a desirable all-sized stand, you must give the same care to harvesting it. Always think of harvesting crop trees as another thinning. Often this will mean cutting trees of questionable quality strictly to ensure that overall quality will improve — or at least remain

Cutting the two trees (indicated) produces only one well-formed tree.

Cutting the middle tree produces two well-formed trees.

Cutting only two of the five trees in the group produces three defective trees from crowding.

Cutting the centre tree as well prevents crowding and produces two well-formed trees.

138

Leave a few seed trees to regenerate the area.

Decide whether you want an all-size stand of trees.

Blocks of even-sized stands are a management alternative.

Fir cone   Fir seedling   Fir seeds

high. Remember that one tree can spoil two or three if left in the stand too long.

SEED TREES

If you are raising wild trees you must consider where the seed will come from for future harvests. If the lot is large, or far from surrounding stands of mature balsam fir, leave a few seed trees. There is no hard-and-fast rule about how many to leave, but three to six per acre (7-15 per hectare) should be sufficient. When selecting seed trees, look for the things you would like to see in your Christmas trees, such as good height growth, dark green colour, good density — preferably double-needled, resistance to disease, and good even whorls with branches between the whorls and five or more branches to each whorl. Where natural seeding fails, you might transplant wild seedlings to fill any large gaps.

STUMP CULTURE

Stump culture is the practice of leaving a whorl or more of live limbs on a stump to produce an additional tree from the old stump. You can do this during thinning or harvesting.

After leaving a couple whorls of limbs, often you will find that a bud has formed near the top of the stump and produced a sprout tree or spike growing straight up. Such a spike will produce a better tree than an upturning limb, and sooner. When this happens, give the spike first choice, but leave several other limbs to feed the old root system.

It is not a good practice to use stump culture in a well-stocked stand. Stump culture should be employed only where trees are scattered and there is little regeneration. Remember that to keep the stump alive you must leave at least one complete whorl. Several would be better.

UNDERPRUNING

Underpruning or butt-pruning removes some or all of the unwanted limbs below the whorl of branches selected as the base of the potential crop tree. This can be done right after weeding and thinning or during shearing, if shearing is planned.

Early butt pruning offers several advantages. If the operator is pressed for time, however, he may omit it for a couple of years in order to complete weeding and thinning the potential stands. Underpruning should be done in advance of any shearing. On the other hand, if a stand is very dense before thinning, and the remaining trees afterwards are thin or spindly, underpruning should be deferred a couple of years.

Underpruning shortens the saleable crown, thereby giving a smaller crop tree. Underpruning too high defeats the purpose. Underprune to correct defects, and establish a handle, not just to make room for regenera-

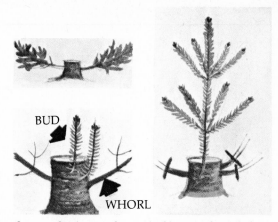

Stump culturing may be practiced in an understocked area. If sprouts develop, favour them over upturning branches.

tion. Six inches on a six foot tree is sufficient for a handle. Another danger in underpruning is the possible damage to the bark. Excessive bark scars will reduce tree vigor. Use a keen axe or hand shears, never a chain saw.

SHEARING

Fast growing stands were avoided by early growers because these produced trees with poor foliage density. Shearing improves density and permits the correction of other defects. This produces saleable trees from those with otherwise poor density, thereby upgrading the number of marketable trees and boosting the productivity and profitability of the operation.

140

Knives or hedge shears are used to shorten leaders and side branches, to bring a lopsided tree into balance, and to stimulate the growth of extra shoots for better density.

The basic rules in shearing fir are: to shear only vigorous trees that need improvement; avoid shearing well-shaped dense trees; start shearing several years before the planned harvest; let at least one year of growth cover the stubs before harvest; shear hardest the first time, correcting small defects later; shear for a cone shape with the base two-thirds the height; work around and around the tree, shearing all faces together and stepping back now and then to inspect the results.

Remember, the general outline of the tree is the important thing. With fir the cuts do not have to be made at a certain point on the twig, as they do with pines. Try instead for an even slope on every face. Normally, an even slope is hard to obtain on the first shearing, especially if it is a heavy one. This is one

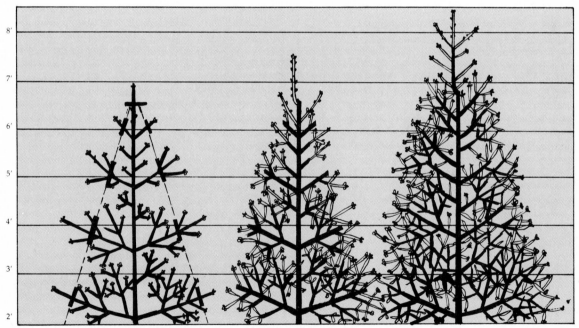

Shearing over a period of years produces a more desirable tree for harvest

reason to start shearing several seasons before harvest — giving the tree time to fill out.

Although the first shearing is usual'y heaviest, it is best to cut no farther into the older growth than necessary. The lower foliage tends to grow more slowly than upper foliage. When the whole tree is sheared heavily, the lower foliage may lag behind the upper crown, producing a top-heavy tree after a few years. Shear more lightly in the lower crown than in the upper, not clipping back beyond the three-year-old growth, if possible.

Leaders should be cut on a slant of about 45 degrees to shed water and promote clean healing. Make the cut about one inch (2.5 centimetres) above a sound side bud. This bud will then become next year's leader. If there are several buds within two to three inches (5 to 7.5 centimetres) of it, pinch them off between thumb and finger if practical. Otherwise they may overtake the new leader and grow into an unsightly cluster of shoots at the top.

The leader should be cut about equal in length to the sheared length of the last whorl of side shoots or laterals. When the top is within arm's reach, a simple way to guage the right length is to bend the laterals up to touch the leader, and cut just above that point. New side buds will normally form on the leader that summer.

The worst features of a tree should be corrected during the first shearing. Later shearings should be mainly to control the new growth. Nevertheless, keep the cone shape in mind, and step back often to check the form.

Take care that a good leader is developing. Before harvest, new growth should be allowed to cover the cut ends and stubs produced by the last shearing. A season's growth is usually enough to do this.

FERTILIZING

Proper use of fertilizer produces greener foliage, longer needles, more buds — which means more branches and denser foliage — and increased height growth. If an untreated stand on a well-drained site is yellowish or shows poor growth, fertilizing usually produces almost unbelievable improvement.

Research findings on the best amounts and types of fertilizer for specific soils and stands are still incomplete. Keep an eye out for developments in tree fertilization.

When you suspect soil problems it is wise to send soil samples for analysis to the Soils and Crops Branch, Nova Scotia Department of Agriculture and Marketing, Truro, N.S. For

Double-needled

Single-needled

soil sample containers and information on techniques, contact your local agricultural representative.

PRE-HARVEST MARKING

When the time comes for the first harvest on a new lot the owner may find it difficult to decide which trees to cut. Unless he learns to organize his harvest beforehand, this could pose problems every fall, especially on the larger lot.

To avoid the problem, invest a few hours of slack time in early fall marking the trees you plan to cut later. Rolls of coloured plastic tape can be used. Tie a short piece to each tree you select, so that you can spot it from the nearest road.

This method provides a second chance at harvest time. If you walk up to a tree and cut it, you have no second choice. Pre-marking the tree for cutting allows you to change your mind later, in case you want to give the tree another year.

The advantages of tagging also include: a basis for estimating the number of marketable trees available each fall; the capability of pre-sorting your trees using different coloured tapes; potential buyers can examine your trees on the stump to good advantage; tagging provides some degree of security for your lot if someone else is cutting the trees. If you do have someone else cutting, however, be sure you fully trust their judgment and skill.

Additional Reading:

Christmas Trees

Managing Wild Balsam Fir for Christmas Trees. Truro, N.S.: Nova Scotia Department of Lands and Forests. 30 pages.

Program for Successfully Establishing Plantations of Balsam Fir for Christmas Trees. Truro, N.S.: Nova Scotia Department of Lands and Forests. 7 pages.

Shearing Fir Christmas Trees. Truro, N.S.: Nova Scotia Department of Lands and Forests. 29 pages.

McLEOD, J. M. *Christmas Tree Management in the Maritime Provinces. Part I: Cultural Practices.* Fredericton, N.B.: Canadian Forestry Service. Maritime Forest Research Centre Information Report M-X-15. 1968. 30 pages.

STIELL, W. M. and C. R. STANTON. *An Introduction to Christmas Tree Growing in Canada.* Ottawa, Ont.: Canadian Forestry Service. Publication Number 1330. 1974. 32 pages.

Shear leaders at a 45-degree angle, about one inch above a healthy bud. Pinch off other buds growing within two or three inches.

9
Woodlot and Wildlife

There are more than just trees in the forest. The forest is a living system in which the trees and other green plants manufacture and provide food for other living members of the forest community. Deer browse on leaves and twigs; earthworms and other soil animals consume fallen leaves and other decaying plant materials; insects feed on plant juices and leaves and they in turn become prey of birds and mammals. Woodland mice eat seeds and insects and they too serve as food for the flesh-eating weasels, hawks and owls.

When plants and animals die, the organisms of decay — bacteria and fungi — break down the tissues into soil nutrients to be recycled by the forest plants. Forests also provide physical shelter for animals and moderate the wind and temperatures.

All animals and plants are part of the complex web of life within the forest ecosytem and all forest animals and plants depend directly or indirectly upon each other for continued existence. The cutting of a tree or removal of an animal affects, albeit to a very small degree, every part of the forest ecosystem.

Recreational activities related to the wildlife resource are enjoyed by as many, if not more,

Nova Scotians than any other form of recreation. At least one fourth of the male population over 14 years old are hunters. One quarter of the total population enjoy sport fishing. Nearly half the households feed birds in winter. Estimated expenditures by wildlife enthusiasts on hunting, fishing, trapping, wildlife viewing, photography, bird feeding and similar activities, in Nova Scotia were $54 million in 1978.

Consideration of wildlife in the woodlot management plan, however, is probably for other than direct economic reasons. Economic benefits of wildlife management accrue indirectly to society, and not always directly to the woodland owner. Concern for wildlife by the woodlot owner is likely to be for some other equally important reason: he gets more enjoyment, satisfaction and a better understanding of nature through managing the woodlot for a variety of purposes; or values the priceless heritage of wildlife and the sense of belonging within a larger web of life.

As with any other crop, good land produces an abundance of wildlife and these lands are the basis of the Nova Scotia wildlife resource. Special areas for wildlife including swamps, marshes and bogs, old depleted

All living things, in the water and above and below ground, form part of the forest ecosystem. Hardwoods encourage wildlife. Even the wildflowers have a place in integrated resource management.

146

fields and pasture lands, bare knolls on hill tops, large gullies, abandoned roads, power-line rights-of-way, gravel and soil pits, steep slopes, and similar areas, are suitable for little other use.

Each of the 40 species of mammals and the more than 140 common species of breeding birds in this province have different food and cover requirements. The abundance of any wildlife species is directly tied to the availability of suitable habitat. There is a limit to the number of individuals of a species that can be produced and supported on a given area of habitat. This limit, the carrying capacity, depends on food, water, cover, behaviour and stress.

Changes in wildlife habitat occur through the natural stages of successional plant growth from bare fields through weed and scrub stages, to pole stage, immature and mature forest and finally overmature forest. Some wildlife species find suitable habitats in the early stages of plant succession while others survive only in the later stages. For the habitat requirements of major game animals in Nova Scotia, see table on pages 150, 151.

Planning for wildlife in the forest may require some change in generally accepted forest management practices. For example, the principal game species, deer, ruffed grouse, snowshoe hare and beaver, require hardwoods. Yet, the tendency in Nova Scotia has been to discourage hardwoods in our forests in favour of softwoods. If one of the landowner's objectives is to increase the species listed in the table, he should plan on cutting practices which favour the regenera-

tion of hardwoods. Most woodland wildlife would benefit from a greater proportion of hardwood and mixedwood types in our forests.

Many of the forest stands in Nova Scotia are evenaged and mature, or nearly so, and therefore too uniform for most wildlife. Plan to correct this situation by patch harvesting smaller areas over an extended period of years to develop a number of age classes and a variety of habitats. Small clearcuts are used

Forests, including dead trees and snags, provide food and shelter for many birds and mammals.

more readily by wildlife than large clearcuts, where there is less protective cover.

The key to wildlife management planning is to provide a variety of habitats that will meet the needs of a variety of wildlife. The more variety, or diversity, the more biologically stable an area will be.

Planning your management for diversity will benefit the woodlot, both for wildlife and wood fibre. A wide variety of stands of various ages, species composition and densities in the forest will be more productive overall than an evenaged forest of one species. The mixed forest tends to be more resistant to insect and disease outbreaks. Increasing hardwoods in the forest reduces forest fire hazard and greatly improves nutrient recycling.

In summary, to support a high wildlife population, woodland must have a plentiful supply of water and suitable year-round food, close to cover which offers protection from enemies and weather.

Following are some of the practices the woodlot owner may undertake in the best general interests of wildlife, and forest, management.

Selection cutting is probably the best single cutting practice for wildlife. It provides branches at various heights in the stand for food and cover, to a variety of animal life. Selection cutting is a desirable cutting system within 50 feet of water courses to protect these very important habitats. The system is best in winter deer yards where it maintains, sufficient crown closure of softwoods for cover. The hardwood component of a stand may be increased through selection cutting. Place emphasis on the develpment of mixedwood stands particularly of tolerant species.

Clearcutting provides food and cover to different wildlife species at different successional stages, and as the stand grows and matures. Most beneficial to wildlife are small clearcuts of one-quarter to one-half acre. Intolerant species such as aspens, white birch and red maple are preferred by deer, snowshoe hare and ruffed grouse. Harvesting intolerant species by strip or patch clearcut methods and clearcutting next to stands of these trees will favour them in the stand. In the same manner, if it is desirable to increase the variety of tree growth in a hardwood stand by encouraging more softwoods, clearcuts can be made adjacent to a seed source of the desired softwoods.

Decaying logs and debris also provide food and shelter for small mammals and other forms of animal life.

148

WILDLIFE SHELTER

A mature softwood stand of about ten acres with about 70 percent crown closure will provide a winter deer yard nucleus, protecting deer from the wind. The closed canopy of softwoods intercepts falling snow to keep ground snow depth shallow enough for deer to move about. Strips of protective cover radiating from this nucleus will extend the area of shallow snow depth enabling deer to travel out in search of hardwood food.

On very cold days, noisy activity of winter cutting operations in or near a deer yard places additional stress on the animals.

Cutting practices may present some conflicts. For example, little thought may be given to leaving hollow den trees or large-crowned overmature wolf trees. Yet these provide den and nesting sites for raccoons, squirrels and many bird species. Similarly, dead trees and snags provide nesting and feeding sites and shelters for birds and mammals. Many of the snag-dependent species represent a major portion of the insect-eating wildlife in the forest. Brush piles, decaying logs and other debris provide food and shelter for small mammals and other forms of animal life.

GREEN BELTS

Aside from provisions of the Forest Improvement Act, it is recommended that green belts be developed and maintained, through selection cuttings within 50 feet of water courses and lakes, to protect important wildlife habitats. Green belts can be encouraged not only along water courses and around lakes, but also on woods roads, trails and highways. Seeding clovers and grasses along woods roads and trails reduces erosion and benefits grazing wildlife. Some woodland openings may be planted for the same purpose. However, do not allow domestic livestock to graze in the woodlot, since they destroy the plant growth on which wildlife depend.

Marshes, swamps and springs or "seeps" are important to wildlife. These areas should be protected from road construction and skid trails as well as from misuse such as waste dumping, draining, filling and similar activities.

Small patch cuts are beneficial to wildlife.

Forestry is a basic resource industry which has a direct and profound influence on wildlife. One careless forest operation can destroy more habitat, eliminate more fish and game, break more nests, move more animals and influence more cover over a longer time than a game manager, with present resources, can create, plant, stock, raise or import in a decade. Conversely, proper techniques applied during the cutting operation will greatly benefit the preferred wildlife species.

The need is to integrate wildlife management with forest management practices.

Managing for wood and wildlife broadens one's perspective of the forest. There is little conflict in integrated resource management when the resources themselves are given primary consideration. But when human demands exceed the ability of resources to produce, the resources are generally sacrificed. Present forest conditions reflect the past policy of money first and resources second. If long term sustained yields of wood, wildlife, water, fish, forest beauty and recreation are to be attained, resource values must be placed above short term economic gains.

HABITAT REQUIREMENTS

Species	Growth Stages Used	Critical Food Source	Other Food Sources
	Herbs, shrubs sapling, pole (mature & immature)	Fir and hardwood browse to ten feet in height	Aquatics, herbaceous plants, etc.
	Herbs, shrubs, sapling, pole (mature)	Hardwood browse herbaecious plants to eight feet in height	Lichens, shrubs, hemlock, fir, etc.
	Herbs, shrubs sapling, pole (mature & overmature)	Wild berries	Fruit, berries, beechnuts, vegetation, animal material, acorns.
	Herbs, shrubs sapling, pole (immature)		Ericaceous plants, shrubs, hardwoods, fir and spruce to eighteen inches above snow cover.
	Sapling, pole (immature, mature & overmature)	Aspens or poplars	Aquatic plants, red maple, ericaceous plants, etc.
	Sapling, pole (immature, mature and overmature)	Aspens and white birch	Fruits, berries, insects and seeds beechnuts

150

Through sound and integrated resource management, it is possible to maintain all of these bounties of nature for the mental and physical well-being of people, without despoiling our priceless heritage of wild birds, fish and animals, and the habitat that supports them. The variety and abundance of fish and wildlife is a primary measure of a healthy forest ecosystem.

Additional Reading:

Wildlife Habitat Improvement Handbook. Washington, D.C., U.S.A.: United States Department of Agriculture. Forest Service Publication FSH 2609.11. 1969.

The Landowner and Wildlife. Kentville, N.S.: Nova Scotia Department of Lands and Forests. 1979.

ELLIOT, R. D. *An Economic Survey of the Use of the Wildlife Resource in Nova Scotia in 1973.* Wolfville, N.S.: Acadia University. B.Sc. Thesis. 1975.

LEOPOLD, ALDO. *Game Management.* New York, U.S.A.: Charles Scribner's Sons. 1947.

PAYNE, F. J. *Toward Integrated Resource Management.* Kentville, N.S.: Nova Scotia Department of Lands and Forests. Extension Note 85. 1974. 11 pages.

PAYNE, F. J. *Wood and Wildlife from Your Woodlot.* Kentville, N.S.: Nova Scotia Conservation. Volume 2, Number 3. 1978.

TELFER, E. S. *Silviculture in the Eastern Deer Yards.* The Forestry Chronicle. August, 1978. Pages 203-208.

HABITAT REQUIREMENTS

Critical Cover Source	Other Cover Sources	Other Needs	Survival in Single Habitat	Approx. Yearly Range in Square Miles
	Topographic features, softwoods, windbreaks	Open patches	No	36
Mature softwood stand, minimum ten acres square	Alder, brushland, immature softwood	Food in or adjacent to cover in winter — sunny open patches	No	36
	Softwood Brushland	Open patches	No	314
Low conifer cover	Poorly stocked (40% crown closure) softwood stands, alder	Open patches	No	0.3
Suitable house site	Alder	Gently flowing stream or lake with food sources; open patches	No	1.0
Conifers, Alders	Brushland, Alder	Open patches	No	1.0

10

Forest Protection

A great many insects and diseases attack forest and shade trees in Nova Scotia. Not all of these cause severe damage. Only a few are discussed here to give the woodland owner some information about the kinds of damage that occur. This may help you to recognize problems and seek appropriate control measures. If you cannot identify a particular problem from the text and illustrations that follow, send a sample of the insect or disease, including a sample of the damage, to the Canadian Forestry Service in Truro.

One of the best preventative measures available to the woodlot owner against insects, is to encourage the development of mixed stands. Good regeneration cutting practices and the practice of silviculture in young stands will decrease the potential for damage.

Among the numerous creatures and conditions attacking the forest (left) are the humble porcupine, spruce budworm larva, tussock caterpillar, wind damage, and careless logging habits.

SPRUCE BUDWORM

The spruce budworm is one of the most damaging forest insect pests in Nova Scotia. Balsam fir and white spruce are the favoured hosts but it also attacks other species.

When the tree's buds begin to swell in the spring the larvae emerge from overwintering nests and begin feeding, mining the needles, buds and male flowers. At this stage the larvae are clay coloured to light brown with a dark brown head.

In late May and throughout June the larvae reach their most conspicuous and damaging stage and are generally pale brown with creamy brown sides and white or yellow spots on their back. About the middle or end of June, they stop feeding and form brown naked pupae. The adult moths emerge about 10 days later.

During severe outbreaks, the larvae may destroy most or all the new foliage and feed into the older foliage. However, the trees will likely succeed in putting out new growth the following year and will recover unless the infestation remains severe for several years. Recovery depends on the vigour of the trees and the severity of the infestation. After three or more years of severe attack, many balsam fir trees may be completely defoliated and begin to die.

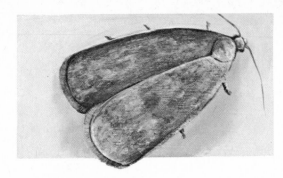

Spruce budworm adult moth.

Spruce budworm larva.

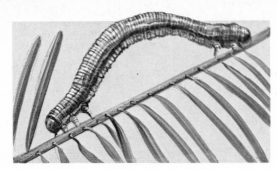

Hemlock looper.

HEMLOCK LOOPER

The hemlock looper is a serious pest in mature and overmature forest stands where balsam fir or hemlock predominate. Large numbers of loopers occur on other species during severe outbreaks.

The young loopers initially feed on the current year's foliage and later in the season on the older needles. Browning of foliage in mid-July is a noticeable feature of an attack. Outbreaks develop quite suddenly and trees may lose over 90 percent of their total foliage in one season and die during the following winter.

WHITEMARKED TUSSOCK MOTH

This insect causes widespread and severe defoliation on both softwoods and hardwoods. Balsam fir, larch and hemlock are the most seriously affected softwoods.

The larvae first skeletonize the leaves of hardwoods, leaving only the leaf veins. Damage to softwoods is typified by brown needles hanging on the underside of the twigs. If trees are seriously defoliated the larvae will migrate and feed on almost any green crop. Fortunately outbreaks eventually collapse from a disease. However, the insect is capable of killing mature and immature stands of fir, and is particularly troublesome in Christmas tree stands.

Whitemarked tussock caterpillar.

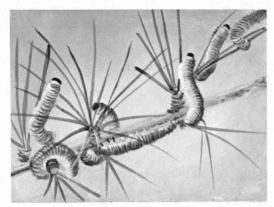

Larch sawfly larvae.

LARCH SAWFLY

The larch sawfly attacks all species of larch. If an attack is heavy, larch sawfly can completely strip a tree and after a few years of heavy defoliation, large trees may die.

The adults lay their eggs in the new shoots of larch causing a characteristic curl which remains for several years as evidence of attack.

EUROPEAN PINE SHOOT MOTH

The European pine shoot moth is a pest of red pine, scots pine and the ornamental mugho pine. The insect is more troublesome on young trees, and serious injury does not occur in forest stands after the canopy has closed.

In late July or August, the half grown larvae enter the buds and overwinter, protected by a resin-encrusted web. In the spring, you can detect the presence of the larvae by the new webs spread between buds or by exuded pitch.

Severe infestations cause the development of adventitious or dormant buds and result in stunted bushy tips and twisted curled branches.

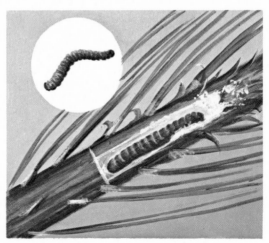

European pine shoot moth.

TENT CATERPILLARS

Two species occur in Nova Scotia. The forest tent caterpillar is the more serious forest pest of the two. It prefers trembling aspen and large areas containing this tree are often completely defoliated. It will also attack oak, apple and other trees. The eastern tent caterpillar feeds chiefly on apple and wild cherry. It is the one that actually forms a "tent".

The caterpillars seldom kill trees, even though they may completely defoliate them. Hardwood trees will usually leaf out again the same year after a severe attack.

Balsam gall midge damage to fir needles.

BALSAM GALL MIDGE

The balsam gall midge can be a troublesome pest to balsam fir Christmas tree growers in Nova Scotia. Most swollen or galled needles become yellow and drop after the larvae have left them in the fall. Severe infestations cause significant defoliation making the trees unfit for the Christmas tree market for several years.

WINTER MOTH

The most important forest host of the winter moth is red oak. The adult moths emerge between late October and early December. The wingless female lays eggs on the trunk and branches. Like the Bruce spanworm, the winter moth larvae are solitary leaf feeders. Trees, moderately to severely defoliated, will put forth new foliage the same season. Once a major forest pest, the insect has been

Forest tent caterpillar.

Eastern tent caterpillar.

157

controlled by the deliberate introduction of parasites.

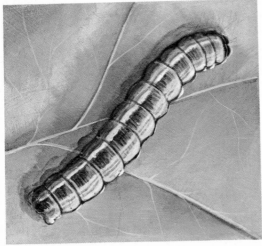

Winter moth larva.

FALL CANKERWORM

The fall cankerworm attacks white elm, red maple, red oak and apple. The life cycle begins in the fall — mid-October to late November — when the wingless female moths crawl up the tree trunks to the branches and twigs to lay eggs. The young larvae eat small holes in the leaves the following spring. Full grown larvae often consume the entire leaf except the mid-rib and larger veins. Severe infestations persist for three or more years, after which the insect is usually brought under control by an egg parasite.

BRUCE SPANWORM

The Bruce spanworm feeds mainly on sugar maple and beech, but also attacks other hardwood trees.

The adults emerge during late October and November, in late afternoon or early evening. The wingless females ascend the trees and mating takes place on the trunks or lower branches. The larvae attack the opening buds and in severe outbreaks can completely defoliate the tree. After a severe attack many species of trees will refoliate the same year. Severe infestations are usually brought under control in about three years by disease of the insect.

Bruce spanworm larva and wingless adult female moths.

Balsam woolly aphid: stem attack (left), gout attack (right).

BALSAM WOOLLY APHID

The balsam woolly aphid attacks balsam fir trees. It reduces the quality and volume of wood and can cause the eventual death of trees.

The aphid causes two types of damage. Feeding on the stem or trunk causes the growth of dense compression wood which reduces wood quality. Patches of white wool-like secretions indicate presence of the insects.

The second form of damage, twig feeding, causes the shoots to swell and become distorted and is commonly referred to as "gout". If attacks persist, bud growth is stopped, height growth is retarded, and the trees slowly die from the top.

BALSAM TWIG APHID

The major host of the balsam twig aphid is the balsam fir. Feeding during May and June, it curls and twists the needles, killing some. Such needles remain deformed as long as they remain on the tree. Heavy infestations mar appearance and can reduce the sale value of Christmas trees. While the trees do not die from heavy aphid infestation, even the healthiest may lose vigour and become subject to other problems.

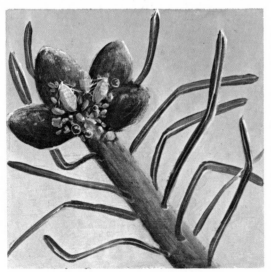

Balsam twig aphid.

Flagging evidence of Dutch elm disease.

DUTCH ELM DISEASE

The Dutch elm disease, accidentally introduced into North America from Europe, was first discovered in Canada in 1944. The fungus causing Dutch elm disease is spread by elm bark beetles. While breeding in diseased elm wood, the insects become covered with spores of Dutch elm disease, then inoculate healthy living trees while seeking new breeding sites.

The first sign of infection is "flagging" in the crown of the elm in late June to early August. The leaves on one or more branches wilt, shrivel and turn yellow. Following these foliar symptoms, the affected branches die, and the condition extends to all other branches and to the stem.

Since the disease is spread from dead or dying trees, the most effective control is "sanitation", that is the removal and destruction of all potential elm bark beetle breeding material. It is not enough to cut off infected branches or cut down dead or dying trees. This elm material must be buried or burned, or all bark removed. A pile of elm logs with bark intact in a back yard, is as inviting a breeding spot as a dying elm tree.

WHITE PINE WEEVIL

This pest is found throughout the range of eastern white pine, damaging eastern white pine and Norway spruce.

The adults go to the terminal shoots to feed and lay eggs in the bark tissues. Resin oozing from feeding punctures on the leader, indicates attack. If the terminal shoot is killed by larvae feeding, it withers, turns red and assumes the shape of a shepherd's crook, revealing the presence of the insect. Then, one or more of the lateral shoots, taking over from the primary terminal shoot, become leaders. This causes the tree to become crooked and forked. Pines grown to sapling height in shade, suffer less damage.

White pine weevil adult.

Terminal shoots killed by feeding larvae.

WHITE PINE BLISTER RUST

White pine blister rust is a disease caused by an introduced fungus. Hosts of this fungus are eastern white pine and wild and/or domestic currants and gooseberries. The fungus alternates between the two hosts and cannot spread directly from pine to pine. Rust spores germinate on currants and gooseberries and are carried by the wind to the pines. The fungus grows into the bark of the pine twig and on down into the branch and trunk. After one to three years, orange-yellow blisters appear on the diseased bark. The blisters produce spores which are carried by the wind to infect currants and gooseberries.

Blister rust can be fatal to white pine at all ages. Trunk cankers, girdling large trees, produce dead tops reducing lumber yields and seriously affecting regeneration.

Right, spore blisters of white pine blister rust.

FIRE CONTROL

The woodlot owner and the operator share the responsibility of taking all the precautions necessary to prevent forest fires from starting and spreading. The Lands and Forests Act covers the liabilities and duties of land owners, occupants and operators with respect to fires starting and spreading on any land, and maintaining fire fighting equipment adequate to the situation. The woodland owner certainly should make himself familiar with the Lands and Forests Act regarding these and other matters.

It is in everyone's interest to prevent forest fires from starting and spreading and every owner should take precautions. An appropriate chemical fire extinguisher should accompany each piece of mechanized equipment. Store one or two back-pack pumps, several fire rakes, shovels, mattocks and axes in one or more places of easy access on the property. Each location should be well marked, FOR FIRE ONLY. Back-packs should be kept in working order and full of water throughout the fire season from early April through October. Your local forester can recommend the number of locations and the type of equipment best suited to your property.

In forest fire control work, time is extremely important. The time it takes for the fire crew to arrive, and the time it takes the owner or other capable person to get to the fire with some hand tools, makes the difference in many cases between putting the fire out in its preliminary stages, and a fire that burns a

good portion of the property.

Brush or other debris should be burned in fall or winter or during wet weather. Check with the Department of Lands and Forests regarding burning permits. Whenever any brush is burned, the back-pack pumps should be kept full and at the scene of the fire for control purposes.

FIRE PONDS

Before building a fire pond, discuss the location and construction of the pond with a forester. Remember, before constructing a pond, approval must be obtained from the Nova Scotia Department of the Environment at Halifax.

Fire ponds should be located in accessible areas where the water table is reasonably high throughout the dry summer months. They should not be located close to a lake or river. Ponds constructed near roads are a great benefit to the fire crew, if a fire breaks out.

The excavation of wet areas such as swamps or bogs, below the water table, is ideal because seepage will keep the ponds full of water and will also benefit the wildlife habitat. The minimum size pond is required to contain 50,000 gallons (230,000 litres) of water. To estimate the capacity in gallons, multiply by six the length in feet, by the width in feet, by the depth in feet (length × width × depth in metres × 1,000 = capacity in litres).

Small fire ponds can be constructed in a number of ways. The first step is to clear the brush and trees from the construction area. This would best be done during a planned harvesting operation. Make sure the cleared area is big enough to receive the soil from the excavation, a 50 foot (15 metre) zone around the pond site is normally enough.

A bulldozer can be used to excavate a shallow pond by pushing the soil material to the side and levelling it afterwards. The excavated soil is piled around the pond and should be pushed back and levelled to some extent before the pond is completed. It would be wise to seed the exposed soil banks with a

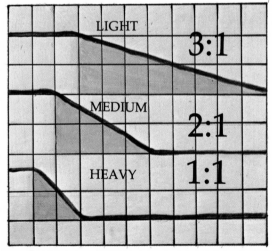

Fire pond: ratio of embankment or dam slopes in relation to different types of soil.

Fire pond dam with overflow pipe.

163

grass seed to prevent erosion back into the pond.

The slope of embankments or dams is important especially on the inside. If you make it too steep for the type of soil, the ground will slump and gully from frost and rain, and may in time break through. For an excavated pond in heavy soils, make the inside slopes to the ratio of 1:1, that is one foot horizontal to one foot vertical.

If the soil is loam or sandy loam, or if the pond has to be built up above natural ground level, make the inside slope about 3:1.

For a constructed dam, slope the upstream face about 3:1, and the downstream face about 2:1. Remember to carry the fill at least 10 per cent higher than the required final height, to allow for settling. The top of the dam should be at least eight feet wide. Provision should be made for overflow by means of a bypass or pipe.

OTHER DAMAGING AGENTS

Not all damage to forest trees is done by insects, diseases or fire. Extremes in climatic conditions, birds, animals and pollution caused by man are responsible for forest losses.

Climatic problems include strong winds, sometimes of hurricane force, which break branches, tops, and blow down trees and forests. In areas subject to strong winds, one should either clearcut mature stands, or cut often and lightly taking out the less windfirm species first. An attempt should be made to

salvage all windfallen trees from your woodlands every year. This should be feasible with a good road system.

Late spring frosts cause damage to trees in frost pockets or low lying areas. The succulent new shoots are frozen, killing the year's growth. Winter drying causes the foliage on spruce and pine trees to turn red, particularly the most recent growth where cold dry winter winds evaporate moisture from the leaders and tips of lateral branches above the snow line. However, this seldom kills trees and the buds usually remain healthy and produce new growth in the spring. Heavy snow and

Sapsucker

Machine damage

Garbage

Bad cutting practices

ice storms cause damage to the weaker stemmed trees. The lower branches of red pine in plantations are often broken by heavy snows in the spring as the snow melts. Ice storms break the stems and branches of hardwood trees, particularly the birches.

Sapsuckers are birds which cause damage to individual trees. The yellow bellied sapsucker sometimes girdles the stem with his holes, killing the portion of the tree above the girdle.

Deer browse young regeneration and can cause serious problems to the regeneration of a forest when their population is too high. Moose also browse the twigs and buds of small trees.

If the tree plantation or woodlot is valuable to the farmstead, all classes of livestock should be fenced out. Cattle and sheep eat off bottom branch tips and rub off the lower branches. Pigs dig up and eat the tree roots, and horses will eat the bark off trees when their diets are incomplete. But, worst of all, livestock will compact the soil in the root area, shutting off good infiltration of moisture and blocking root respiration.

Rodent pests include our rabbits or snowshoe hares, mice and porcupines. Keeping the plantation free of weeds and trash is the best way to reduce rodent damage. Thick grass attracts mice; weed and brush piles attract hares. A clean planting should not be bothered by mice, but neighboring hares can still reduce the young trees to stubs.

Roadside salt spray causes much damage to foliage, with many trees dying along highways. White pine and sugar maple are particularly susceptible. Fumes from the thermal generating stations and oil refineries also are known to kill nearby trees.

Perhaps the worst damage to the forest environment is caused by careless logging. Tree trunks and roots are frequently scarred by the wheels of tractors and skidders. These wounds often develop into butt rot or other defects which lower the value of trees. Rutting and erosion of landscapes are another problem, if logging is carried out in the spring when soils are saturated with water.

Additional Reading:

Tree Pest Control Leaflets. Fredericton, N.B.: Canadian Forestry Service. Maritime Forest Research Centre.

BAKER, W. L. *Eastern Forest Insects.* Washington, D.C., U.S.A.: United States Department of Agriculture. Forest Service Miscellaneous Publication 1175. 1972. 642 pages.

BEDARD, J. R. *The Small Forest and the Tree Farm. Book III - Woodlot Development and Protection.* Fredericton, N.B.: New Brunswick Department of Agriculture and Rural Development. 1968.

DAVIDSON, A. G. and R. M. PRENTICE (editors). *Important Forest Insects of Mutual Concern to Canada, the United States and Mexico.* Ottawa, Ont.: Canada Department of Forestry and Rural Development. Publication number 1180. 1967. 248 pages.

VAN SICKLE, G. A. *A Field Manual of Tree Diseases in the Maritimes.* Fredericton, N.B.: Canadian Forestry Service. Maritime Forest Research Centre Information Report M-X-1. 1966.

Forest Fire Control in Canada. Ottawa, Ont.: Canadian Forestry Service. Catalogue number F061/3/75. 1974. 32 pages.

Building Woodland Ponds. Truro, N.S.: Nova Scotia Department of Lands and Forests. 21 pages.

Appendix I

The Forest Improvement Act

CHAPTER 114, REVISED STATUTES OF NOVA SCOTIA 1967, AS AMENDED.

This consolidation has been made for the convenience of the Department of Lands and Forests only and is not a Statutory Revision.

Excerpt from

THE FOREST IMPROVEMENT ACT

Chapter 7 of the Statutes of Nova Scotia

1965

Preamble   WHEREAS the public welfare of Nova Scotia requires the maintenance, protection and rehabilitation of the forests and of the productivity of forests lands to

(a) provide continuous and increasing supplies of forest products thereby maintaining forest industries and providing continued employment;

(b) conserve water and prevent or reduce floods; and

(c) improve conditions for wildlife, recreation and scenic values;

Therefore, be it enacted by the Governor and Assembly as follows:

CHAPTER 114

Forest Improvement Act

Interpretation
1 In this Act,

(a) "buyer" means a person who as principal or agent or otherwise acquires a primary forest product of a commercial forest operation;

(b) "commercial forest operation" means an operation involving the cutting or felling of trees for primary forest products but does not include.

(i) the cutting or felling of trees for fuel wood; or

(ii) an operation by a proprietor or wood lot owner who employs not more than two helpers in a cutting operation of less than twenty-five thousand feet board measure or fifty cords or an equivalent volume by any other method of measurement on his own wood lot or farm in any calendar year;

(c) "Department" means Department of Lands and Forests;

(d) "Forest Practices Improvement Board" or "Board" means a board appointed by the Governor in Council pursuant to this Act;

(e) "forest district" means an area described and defined as a forest district by the Minister;

(f) "immature stand" means an area of not less than three acres of young healthy spruce, pine, hemlock or yellow birch which according to the criteria established as a result of studies carried out by the Minister pursuant to subsection (3) of Section 9 is an immature stand;

(ff) "lake" or "designated lake" means a lake designated by the Governor in Council pursuant to this Act as a designated lake;

(g) "Minister" means Minister of Lands and Forests;

(h) "operator" means a person who carries on or causes to be carried on a commercial forest operation;

(i) "primary forest product" means any part or parts of commercial value of a tree which has been felled but has not been processed beyond removing the limbs or bark or both;

(j) "river" or "designated river" means a river or a portion thereof designated by the Governor in Council pursuant to this Act as a designated river;

(k) "spruce" means red and black spruce. 1965, c. 7, s. 1, 1968, c. 28, s.1.

Buyer's certificate of registration.

2 (1) No person shall buy or otherwise acquire except by inheritance or other process of law a primary forest product except for his personal use or consumption or for fuel wood unless he holds a buyer's certificate of registration issued by the Minister under this Act.

Operator's certificate of registration

(2) No person shall conduct a commercial forest operation unless he holds an operator's certificate of registration issued by the Minister under this Act. 1965, c. 7, s. 2.

Issue of certificates.

3 (1) Subject to the regulations, the Minister may issue certificates of registration.

Cancellation or suspension of certificates.

(2) The Minister may cancel or suspend for such period as he thinks advisable the certificate of registration of any buyer or operator convicted of an offence under this Act.

Duration and renewal of certificates.

(3) Every certificate is valid for the calendar year in which it is issued and, upon application, shall be renewed from year to year so long as the holder makes the reports and returns required under this Act and has not been convicted of an offence under this Act. 1965, c. 7, s. 3.

Records and reports by buyers and operators.

4 Every holder of a certificate of registration issued under this Act shall keep such records and make such reports and reports and returns as are prescribed or required by the regulations. 1965, c. 7, s. 4.

Proof of registration.

5 A certificate signed or purporting to be signed by the Minister and bearing the seal of the Department that on a date or within a period stated in the certificate a person was or was not the holder of a certificate of registration under this Act or did not file a report as required by this Act or the regulations shall be received in evidence without proof of the signature or of the official character of the person appearing to have signed it and shall be *prima facie* proof of the facts stated therein. 1965, c. 7, s. 5.

Provincial Board established

5A (1) There shall be a Provincial Forest Practices Improvement Board for the Province, consisting of seven members,

(a) one of whom shall be the Minister or a person appointed by the Minister who shall act as Chairman of the Provincial Board; and

(b) six of whom shall be appointed by the Governor in Council to represent the following; namely.

(i) the Nova Scotia Voluntary Planning Board,

(ii) the sawn products segment of the forest industry,

(iii) the pulp products segment of the forest industry,

(iv) the owners of small woodlots,

(v) the Nova Scotia Section of the Canadian Institute of Forestry, and

(vi) the Nova Scotia Wildlife Federation

Term of office of members.

(2) The Governor in Council may prescribe the term of office of each member of the Provincial Board appointed pursuant to clause (b) of subsection (1).

Secretary and executive officer.

(3) The Minister shall appoint an officer employed in the Department to act as secretary and executive officer of the Provincial Board.

Functions and duties.

(4) The function of the Provincial Board shall be to encourage better forest practices in the Province and the Provincal Board shall:

(a) do everything in its power to encourage better forest management practices through education, persuasion and enforcement of this Act and the regulations;

(b) with the approval of the Minister, cause to be prepared a manual of good forest practice;

(c) tender the manual or make it available to operators and buyers in the Province;

(d) make available to operators and buyers the forms prescribed for making their reports and returns;

(e) prescribe, advise and make recommendations concerning cutting practices and reforestation procedures in the Province;

(f) work closely and in co-operation with representatives of the Department;

(g) assist, co-operate with, foster and initiate activity by the Forest Practices Improvement Boards;

(h) co-ordinate the activities of the Forest Practices Improvement Boards by establishing and maintaining contact with each Board;

(i) establish educational and other programs for the benefit of persons engaged or interested in the forest industry;

(j) report annually to the Governor in Council on the activities of the Provincial Forest Practices Improvement Board and the Forest Practices Improvement Boards appointed for forest districts and make recommendations for improvement of the administration of this Act.

Expenses of members.	(5) Members of the Provincial Board other than the Minister shall be paid by the Department such reasonable and necessary expenses as are incurred by them in carrying out their functions under this Act and may be reimbursed at such rate and in such manner as the Governor in Council determines. 1968, c. 28, s. 2.
Designation of forest district.	**6** The Minister may by order published in the Royal Gazette designate and describe an area as a forest district for the purposes of this Act. 1965, c. 7, s. 6.
Appointment of Boards.	**7** (1) The Governor in Council may appoint for any forest district a Forest Practices Improvement Board consisting of a representative of the Department and not more than ten other persons representing so far as is practicable, the following interests; namely, small wood lot owners, the owners of woodlands of one thousand acres or more, the municipalities included within the district, on a rotational basis if necessary, and one member at large.
Term of office of members.	(2) The Governor in Council may prescribe the term of office of each member of a Board and may designate one member to be chairman.
Status of forester.	(3) The representative of the Department who is a member of the Board shall act as technical adviser and may act as secretary unless another member is appointed by the Board.
Reimbursement of Board members.	(4) The members of a Board shall be paid by the Department such reasonable and necessary expenses as are incurred by them in carrying out their functions under this Act and may be reimbursed at such rate and in such manner as the Governor in Council determines. 1965, c. 7, s. 7, 1968, c. 28, s. 3.
Functions of Board.	**8** The Governor in Council may, upon such terms and conditions as he deems fit and necessary, delegate to a Forest Practices Improvement Board for a forest district, such of the powers, within that forest district, of the Provincial Forest Practices Improvement Board as the Governor in Council deems necessary for the proper administration of this Act and may, at any time, terminate such delegation of power.
Felling of immature trees.	**9** (1) Except for the purpose of providing necessary roadways or brow or camp sites no person, as part of a commercial forest operation, shall fell healthy immature spruce, pine hemlock or yellow birch trees in an immature stand of any of such species unless he has first obtained permission to do so from the Board of the district in which the stand is situated.

Determination of immaturity.	(2) On an application for permission under this Section the Board with such advice as it considers necessary or advisable will determine whether or not the stand is an immature stand and will use its best judgment in establishing a satisfactory criterion for maturity and whether and upon what conditions having regard to all relevant circumstances such permission should be granted.
Studies by Minister.	(3) In order to help achieve a satisfactory criterion, the Minister may carry out scientific studies to ascertain the point of economic culmination and growth on average stands at which the peak of potential yield or volume can be expected or the stage of growth at which a given acre will on the average produce the greatest volume of wood, and the Board in making a judgment under subsection (2) shall give due weight to the findings of such a study.
Idem.	(4) The Minister shall ensure that the studies mentioned in subsection (3) are carried out in all reasonable consultation with representatives of the Nova Scotia Voluntary Planning Board, the Nova Scotia Forest Products Association, the Nova Scotia Section of the Canadian Institute of Forestry, the Nova Scotia Wildlife Federation, the Small Woodlot Owners' Association and the Nova Scotia Section of the Canadian Forestry Association.
Cutting practices.	**10** (1) A person who is carrying on a commercial forest operation shall not fell or cause to be felled trees in any stand except in accordance with practices recommended by the Board for the district in which the stand is situated.
Duty of Board.	(2) The Board in prescribing or recommending cutting practices shall require that cutting be carried out in such manner as to promote the likelihood of regeneration and preserve existing young growth of desirable species of trees.
Injunctions, application for.	(3) When in the opinion of the Minister a forest-cutting operation is being carried on in such a manner as is clearly likely substantially to destroy the future potential of the stand on which it is being carried on or its normal regeneration the Minister, with the approval of the Governor in Council, may apply to the judge of the County Court having jurisdiction in the place where the stand is for an injunction is to restrain the further carrying on of the operation.
Procedure.	(4) The judge shall as soon as reasonably possible hear the application and may grant or refuse it upon such terms as appear to him to be just and reasonable in accordance with the general law and rules of court relating to injunctions.
Appeal from judge.	(5) An appeal shall lie from the decision of the judge of the County Court to the Appeal Division of the Supreme Court.

Costs.	(6) Upon the hearing of an application or an appeal under this Section, the judge of the County Court or the Appeal Division of the Supreme Court may award costs against the Minister but not against the defendant. 1965, c. 7, s. 10.
Duties of commercial operator.	**11** (1) The person conducting any commercial forest operation shall use every effort to harvest all possible saleable wood of commercial value contained in tops, stumps, fir and other like species and diseased wood.
Powers of Board re commercial operators.	(2) When in the opinion of the Board for the district in which an operation was carried on the person conducting the operation has not complied with subsection (1) and a market exists for the wood that was not harvested that will afford sufficient remuneration to cover the normal cost of harvesting and transportation by reasonably efficient methods appropriate to the size and nature of the operation and the location of the market, the Board may require the operator within a reasonable time to be prescribed by the Board to harvest wood that was not harvested in the original operation and that is specified in the order of the Board.
Disobedience of Board order.	(3) A person who without reasonable grounds fails to obey an order of a Board given under subsection (2) is guilty of an offence under this Act.
Principles to be observed by Board.	(4) The Board in carrying out its duties shall give appropriate weight to the principle that all trees cut will be used as far as reasonably practicable for the purpose which will best contribute to the sustained development of the economy of the Province. 1965, c. 7, s. 11.
Green belt on highways, rivers and lakes.	**12** (1) No person shall fell a tree within one hundred feet of

(a) the outside boundary of any trunk highway or such other highway as is designated by the Governor in Council; or

(b) the bank of any designated river, part of river or lake;

except for the purpose of providing roadways or brow sites or except with the approval of the Board and under the conditions prescribed by the Board and under the supervision of the Board's forester.

Permitted cutting.	(2) When an application is made to a Board under subsection (1) the Board shall approve the cutting under supervision of mature trees or of any trees or thinning or select cutting on condition that all reasonable precautions are taken to minimize fire hazard and to maintain a green border of healthy growing trees along the margin of the highway or designated river or lake.

(3) The Governor in Council may designate any river in the Province or any portion of a river as a designated river or any lake as a designated lake for the purposes of this Section and of this Act. 1965, c. 7, s. 12.

Regulations.

13 The Minister, subject to the approval of the Governor in Council and after all reasonable consultation with representatives of the organizations mentioned in subsection (4) of Section 9, may make regulations:

(a) prescribing the records to be kept and maintained by buyers and operators and the forms of reports and returns and the information to be contained therein to be made by buyers and operators;

(b) prescribing the time or times at which reports and returns shall be made;

(c) prescribing the forms of certificates of registration and the manner and form of making application therefor;

(d) prescribing the terms, conditions and restrictions to which certificates of registration may be subject;

(e) prescribing the fees payable for certificates of registration and the time of payment thereof;

(f) prescribing the amounts of loans that may be made by the Timber Loan Board and the terms and conditions upon which such loans may be made;

(g) prescribing the procedure to be followed in any appeal to the Minister from a decision of a Board;

(h) respecting any other matter indicated in this Act. 1965, c. 7, s. 13, 1968, C. 28, s. 5.

Penalties.

14 A person who violates or fails to observe any provision of this Act or the regulations or an order or direction of a Board given under this Act is guilty of an offence and upon conviction for a

(a) first offence may be ordered to pay the costs of the prosecution and, until the Minister orders otherwise, shall not be eligible to receive any assistance of any kind from or through the Department or the Timber Loan Board or to engage in any transaction of any kind relating to Crown lands except as a *bona fide* employment as an individual wage earner; and

(b) second or subsequent offence is liable in addition to any penalty that may be imposed under clause (a) and the disqualification arising under that clause to the penalty prescribed by Section 89 of the Summary Convictions Act. 1965, c. 7, s. 14.

Consent to prosecution.	**15** No prosecution under this Act shall be instituted except with the written consent of the Minister. 1965, c. 7, s. 15.
Appeal from Board.	**16** Any person affected by a decision of a Board may appeal from the decision to the Minister. 1965, c. 7, s. 16.
Timber Loan Board.	**17** (1) There is hereby established a Timber Loan Board, the chairman, members and staff of which shall be the persons who from time to time are the chairman, members and staff of the Nova Scotia Farm Loan Board.
Loans by Board.	(2) The Timber Loan Board may make loans to persons for the purchase of forest lands in such amounts and upon such terms and conditions as may be prescribed by regulations made pursuant to Section 13.
Financing of Board.	(3) The authority contained in the Agriculture and Rural Credit Act for the provision of funds for the use of the Nova Scotia Farm Loan Board shall extend and be applicable to and the authority of the provision of funds for the use of the Timber Loan Board in making loans and in defraying its expenses. 1965, c. 7, s. 17.
Assessment of reforested lands.	**18** Notwithstanding the provisions of the Assessment Act or of any other Act, land that is planted with trees in accordance with practices recommended by a Board pursuant to this Act shall not until after a period of twenty years has elapsed from the date of such planting be assessed for a greater amount than that for which it was assessed immediately before such planting, except as may be necessary to compensate for changes in the value of money or to maintain its assessment in the proper relation to the assessment of other lands where there has been a general re-assessment of property throughout the municipality in which the lands are situated. 1965, c. 7, s. 18.
Effective dates.	**19** The individual Sections of this Act shall come into force on and not before such date and in such part or parts of the Province as the Governor in Council from time to time orders and declares by proclamation. 1965, c. 7, s. 21.

Appendix II

Guidelines to Sections 9, 10, 11 and 12 of The Forest Improvement Act

SECTION 9: GUIDELINES

The objectives of Section 9, of the Forest Improvement Act, as it applies to commercial forest operations are as follows:

a To maintain and protect healthy stands of red and black spruce, pine, hemlock and yellow birch which are growing vigorously and are still immature.

b To provide for future continuous supplies of forest products.

c To promote good forestry practices throughout the province.

The Provincial Forest Practices Improvement Board has accepted, for the purpose of the Act, an immature stand of desirable species as one:

1 not less than 3 acres in size;

2 consisting of vigorous and healthy trees of an age, height, species make up and density to be different with respect to these features from surrounding forests;

3 with more than 50 per cent of the volume in red or black spruce or pine or hemlock or yellow birch or mixtures of these species;

4 falling into one of the following:
(a) less than 60 years of age at breast height;
(b) having an average stand diameter of less than seven inches diameter at breast height.

If by these guidelines a stand appears to be immature it should receive the attention of the Board before being cut. If a stand is not immature by these guidelines then it may be cut without permission of the Board. This is not to imply that it is a mature stand and should be cut. There are indicators of maturity which can be used in making this decision (see page 26).

For the purposes of determining immaturity as used in this Act, the following procedure will be used:

1 The average stand diameter is determined on the basis of the measurement of all trees 3.6 inches and over in diameter at breast height on a one-tenth acre plot located at random within each one-quarter of the total stand area (see page 40 line 4).

2 Age is determined at breast height on one or two representative dominant or codominant trees per plot and averaged for the stand.

175

SECTION 10: GUIDELINES

The objectives of Section 10, of the Forest Improvement Act, as it applies to commercial forest operations are as follows:

a   To keep forest lands in a productive state occupied with trees of such species, vigour, and stages of growth that a continuous supply of forest products may be realized.

b   To promote, primarily through cutting practices, the likelihood of regeneration of desirable species of trees.

c   To protect existing young growth of desirable species of trees.

d   To carry out felling operations in such a manner that aesthetic, wildlife, watershed, and forest protection features are given proper consideration.

The following cutting practice guidelines are suggested:

1   "Stands" with considerable advance regeneration of "desirable species" should be cut with care and in such a way that a goodly number of healthy undamaged tree seedlings or saplings of "desirable species" remain well distributed in the area once the cutting is completed. The size and shape of the cut, particularly any clearcut, should be influenced by wildlife considerations, natural boundaries, appearances, and the forestry practices of the adjacent landowners.

2   "Stands" without advance regeneration of "desirable species" which are planned for clearcutting should be cut in strips or patches.

3   "Stands" with or without advance regeneration of "desirable species" may also be cut by the selection system or the shelterwood system favouring the retention of "desirable species". An effort should be made to prevent root and bark damage to residual trees from skidding operations in partial cuts.

4   Where adequate natural regeneration does not develop within a reasonable time after clearcutting, reforestation should be undertaken using species suitable to the site.

5   Consideration should be given to postponing the cutting operation until just after a good seed year for "desirable species" occurs.

6   Nothing in these guidelines prevents the harvesting of dying, dead or blown down trees.

SECTION 11: GUIDELINES

The objectives of Section 11, of the Forest Improvement Act, as it applies to commercial forest operations are as follows:

a   To promote good utilization of wood fibre in harvesting operations throughout the province.

b   To reduce excessive waste in tree tops, stumps and harvest operations throughout the province.

c   To promote the concept that good quality sawlog material be used for the production of lumber.

d   To promote utilization practices that will best contribute to the sustained development of the economy of the province.

The following utilization practices are suggested as guidelines:

1. When felling any tree, the remaining stump, if it contains sound wood, should have a height of less than 10 inches (25 centimetres) above the ground.
2. No merchantable part of a felled tree that can be economically harvested and marketed should remain on the site after a commercial operation.
3. Preference should be given to the harvest of dying, dead or blown down merchantable trees.
4. Merchantable wood should be removed from the forest and should not be left at landings and along roadsides after an operation is completed.

SECTION 12: GUIDELINES

The objectives of Section 12 of the Forest Improvement Act as it applies to designated highways, rivers and lakes are:

a. To maintain designated highways, riverbanks, and lakeshores in an aesthetically pleasing condition;
b. To maintain a sufficient forest cover on the areas bordering designated rivers and lakes to control water runoff, reduce erosion, and stabilize the banks;
c. To provide shading over the designated water to moderate water temperatures and improve fish habitat; and
d. To provide shelter for wildlife along the designated shorelines.

This Section of the Forest Improvement Act applies to all tree cutting whether in commercial forest operations or not.

The following guidelines are prescribed by the Provincial Forest Practices Improvement Board for designated highways, rivers and lakes under Section 12 of the Forest Improvement Act to meet these objectives.

These guidelines apply to woodland situations only, and not to ornamental trees adjacent to dwellings, nor to trees maintained for the production of fruit crops.

1. Applications for permission to fell trees within the 100-foot strip bordering designated highways, rivers and lakes shall be directed by the person proposing to do the felling to the forestry personnel acting on behalf of the Board.
2. Forestry personnel acting on behalf of the Board may inspect the area on which cutting is proposed to take place, in company with the applicant, and shall recommend cutting practices based upon the guidelines contained herein.

SPECIFIC CONDITIONS APPLICABLE TO DESIGNATED RIVERS AND LAKES

1. Trees providing shade over designated lakes or rivers shall not be cut, unless for an exceptional reason acceptable to the forestry personnel acting on behalf of the Board.
2. In general, within the designated area of the greenbelt, all cutting approved shall be on an individual tree selection basis only leaving an adequate stand of trees to

be wind-firm and provide a continuous forest cover; only mature and overmature trees may be cut.

3   When the slope of the shoreline is excessive (greater than 30 per cent) these conditions should be extended to 150 feet on the sloping side(s) of the designated river or lake, or more as the forestry personnel and applicant see fit.

4   When trees are cut, felling is to be away from the river or lake so that the tops or branches will not fall in the water; any logging debris entering the water should be removed; and care should be taken to prevent any damage to the banks or bed of the designated river or lake.

5   Walking trails and canoe carries within the designated area should be kept clear of brush and tops resulting from cutting operations.

6   Skidding trails shall be located at such angles to the banks of rivers or lakes as to prevent rapid run-off and subsequent erosion and siltation; no machinery is to be used within 66 feet of the bank of any designated river or lake, and diversion ditches must be provided on slopes to prevent gully erosion.

7   Felling and hauling of trees cut should be done in such a manner as to minimize damage to the remaining stand of trees, and roads and culverts shall be built only where necessary and with due care to their effect on the passage of fish and wildlife.

SPECIFIC CONDITIONS APPLICABLE TO DESIGNATED HIGHWAYS

1   The maximum distance which may be clearcut parallel with the highway for a brow or yarding area is 150 feet.

2   Subject to the exceptions listed in the Forest Improvement Act, and to those listed in these conditions, the felling of any tree within 100 feet (30 metres) of the outside boundary of any designated highway will not be approved until its diameter at breast height is 10 inches or larger.

3   Approval for the clearcutting of any stand within 100 feet of the outside boundary of a designated highway will not be given unless one of the following conditions is met:

(i)   There is well-established and well-distributed regeneration on the area to be clearcut to the extent of at least 1,000 stems per acre of any tree species.

(ii)   The landowner agrees to allow planting to be carried out under the direction of the Board if suitable natural regeneration is not established within five years following cutting.

(iii)   The land involved is to be changed to a non-forest use.

4   In situations where the appearance of the stand, the characteristics of the species involved, or other evidence, such as the presence of butt-rot, indicates that trees should be felled to a smaller size than 10

inches at breast height, then approval for such felling may be given.

5   In situations where the felling of trees 10 inches or larger, in diameter at breast height, will result in leaving smaller trees in a condition such that they, in all probability, will blow down, or where the best forestry practice dictates that the whole stand, or a portion thereof, be felled, then approval for such felling may be given.

6   Fellings in the nature of cleanings, thinnings, and the salvage of defective trees will be approved for all species before reaching the size of 10 inches in diameter.

   Also, where stands are being managed for commercial Christmas tree production, fellings will be approved before the size of 10 inches in diameter is reached.

7   Approval may be given for felling trees before they reach 10 inches in diameter where the view from the highway of an aesthetically pleasing feature is distinctly improved by doing so.

8   With the object of establishing variation in the forest stands bordering designated highways the maximum continuous distance allowed to be clear-felled on any one ownership within a five year period is 1,000 feet.

   In certain circumstances, because of the proximity of boundary lines, the occurrence of insect or disease infestations or the characteristics of the forest stand, the Board may approve the clear-felling of distances in excess of 1,000 feet.

9   With the object of minimizing brush along the highways, when cutting is approved, trees are to be felled back at right angles to the road boundary wherever possible.

10 When cutting is being carried out all branches and tops of trees shall be cut into portions so that the general level of the brush is not higher than two feet above the ground level.

11 When cutting is being carried out it is to be done in a manner so as to leave the area adjacent to the highway neat and with as pleasant an appearance as possible.

12 Because of the beauty of hardwoods bordering the highways, and because of their value in fire control, forest owners are encouraged to leave hardwoods growing wherever possible.

Appendix III

Table of Map Scales and Conversions

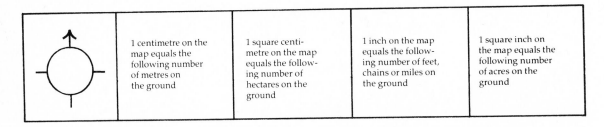

	1 centimetre on the map equals the following number of metres on the ground	1 square centimetre on the map equals the following number of hectares on the ground	1 inch on the map equals the following number of feet, chains or miles on the ground	1 square inch on the map equals the following number of acres on the ground
1: 5000	50 m	0.25 ha	416.67 ft 6.31 ch 0.789 mi	3.98 acres
1: 6000	60 m	0.36 ha	500 ft 7.57 ch 0.947 mi	5.74 acres
1:10000	100 m	1 ha	833.33 ft 12.63 ch 0.158 mi	15.95 acres
1:12000	120 m	1.44 ha	1000 ft 15.15 ch 0.189 mi	22.95 acres
1:15000	150 m	2.25 ha	1250 ft 18.94 ch 0.237 mi	35.87 acres
1:15840	158.4 m	2.51 ha	1320 ft 20 ch 0.25 mi	40 acres
1:20000	200 m	4 ha	1666.67 ft 25.25 ch 0.316 mi	63.76 acres
1:50000	500 m	7.5 ha	4166.67 ft 63.13 ch 0.789 mi	398.54 acres
1:63360	633.6 m	40.14 ha	5280 ft 80 ch 1 mi	640 acres

Appendix IV

Sample Management Plan

Property Map of John Doe Farm
Lot 5280, County of Annapolis, N.S.

Prepared by John Doe November 1979

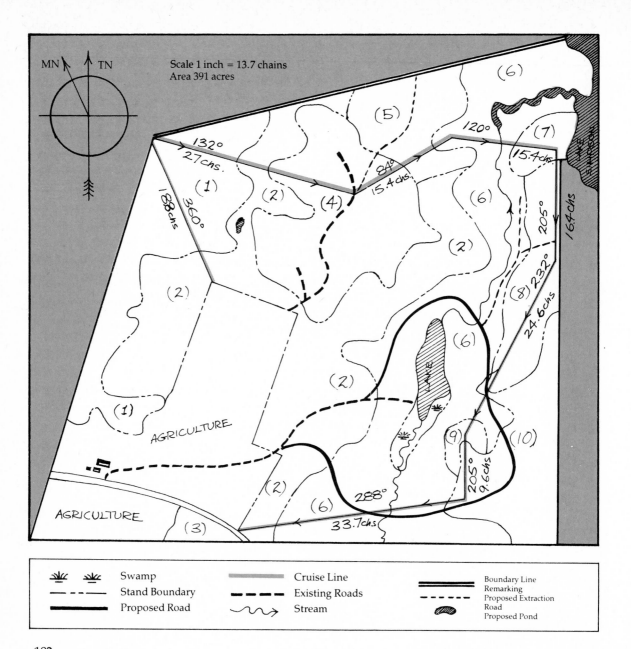

Scale 1 inch = 13.7 chains
Area 391 acres

MN   TN

AGRICULTURE

AGRICULTURE

LAKE

LAKE SIMCOM

Swamp	Cruise Line	Boundary Line Remarking
Stand Boundary	Existing Roads	Proposed Extraction Road
Proposed Road	Stream	Proposed Pond

Woodland Management Stand Assessment Sheet

1. Line number or Bearing	360°	132°		132°	84°
2. Stand number	(1)	(2)	(3)	(4)	(5)
3. Area (acres)	37	84	3	34	17
4. Average Diameter (inches)	6	10	—	1	5
5. Average Age	50	70	—	5-10	50
6. Average Height (feet)	52	75	—	7	50
7. Forest Capability	5	4	—	—	5
8. Maturity	3	4,5	—	2	3-4
9. Density	2	3	—	4	3
10. Drainage	2	3	2	3	3
11. Windfirmness	1	2	—	1	2
12. Species Composition	5sM 4rM 1H	4rS,2wP 2bF,2rM	—	4rS,4wP 2bF	7bS,2bF 1rS
13. Cover type	3	1	11	1	1
14. Wildlife Habitat Features	3,4	4,11,12	12	4,11,12	6,11,12
15. Products	6,4,2	2,3,4	—	7(some)	2,3
16. Treatments	10,3	3,4	8	9	2
17. Priority	1	1	1	1	1
18. Average Stand Basal Area (sq. feet/acre)	90	150	—	—	130
Basal Area Desirable Species	20	50	—	—	100
19. Gross Merchantable Volume (cubic feet)					
Total	1575	4500	—	—	2275
Pulpwood: SW	160	675	—	—	2048
HW	1415	450	—	—	—
Sawlogs: SW	—	2925	—	—	227
HW	—	450	—	—	—
Desirable Species only	160	2700	—	—	1750
20. Non-merchantable Volume: SW	—	—	—	—	—
HW	—	—	—	—	—
21. Regeneration					
Species Composition	8sM,1yB 1H	4rS,4bF 2sM	—	4rS,4wP 2bF	7bS,2bF 1rS
Stocking	M	I	—	O	I
Height	2"-1'	2"-1'	—	5'-10'	0-1'-1.0'

183

Woodland Management Stand Assessment Sheet

	(6)	(7)	(8)	(9)	(10)
1. Line number or Bearing	84°	120°	205°	232°	205°
2. Stand number	(6)	(7)	(8)	(9)	(10)
3. Area (acres)	109	5	15	2	22
4. Average Diameter (inches)	5	—	8	4	—
5. Average Age	45	—	70	30	3
6. Average Height (feet)	35	—	65	26	6
7. Forest Capability	6	—	4	6	—
8. Maturity	3	2	3,4	3	1-2
9. Density	2	—	3	2	1
10. Drainage	3-4	4	2	1	2
11. Windfirmness	2	1	1	1	1
12. Species Composition	6bF, 2rS 2rM	6S	5rS, 4wP 1rM	4rS, 3wP 3sM	rM
13. Cover type	1	9	1	2	4
14. Wildlife Habitat Features	2,4,5,6,11	2,13	11,12	3,4,6,12	11,12
15. Products	2,3,4	—	2,34	2,3,4	—
16. Treatments	1	1	5	wildlife	7
17. Priority	2+	4	1	4	1
18. Average Stand Basal Area (sq. feet/acre)	105	—	130	90	—
Basal Area Desirable Species	26	—	110	60	—
19. Gross Merchantable Volume (cubic feet)					
Total	1050	—	3250	—	—
Pulpwood: SW	578	—	487	—	—
HW	210	—	325	—	—
Sawlogs: SW	262	—	2438	—	—
HW	—	—	—	—	—
Desirable Species only	210	—	2750	473	—
20. Non-merchantable Volume: SW	—	—	—	473	—
HW	—	—	—	202	—
21. Regeneration					
Species Composition	4bF, 3rS 3rM	6S	3rS, 36F 2wP, 2rM	4bF, 2rS 2wP, 1H, 1sM	rM
Stocking	A	I	I	I	I-M
Height	1'-5'	1'-5'	0-1'-1'	1'-5'	1'-5'

TABLE 1: LAND CLASSIFICATION

Productive Forest	Acres	%	Non-Productive Forest	Acres	%	Non-forested	Acres	%
Softwood	259	66	Old field	3	1	Agricultural	59	15
Mixedwood	2	1	Bogs	—	—	Old fields	—	—
Hardwood	37	9	Swamp			Bogs	—	—
Christmas trees	—	—	Water			Swamp	4	1
Sugarwoods	—	—	Other			Water	5	1
Other	—	—				Other	—	—
Cutover	22	6						
Total	320	82	Total	3	1	Total	68	17
Grand Total	391	100						

TABLE 2: PRODUCTIVE FOREST LAND AREA BY AGE CLASS

Age Class (Years)	Softwood	Mixedwood	Hardwood	Total	%
Areas not regenerating satisfactorily	—	—	22	22	7
I 1-15 years	34	—	—	34	10
II 16-30 years	—	2	—	2	1
III 31-45 years	109	—	—	109	34
IV 46-60 years	17	—	37	54	17
V 61-75 years	99	—	—	99	31
VI 76-90 years	—	—	—	—	
VII 91+ years	—	—	—	—	
Uneven Aged	—	—	—	—	
Total (%)	259 (81)	2 (1)	59 (18)	320	100

TABLE 3: FIVE YEAR HARVEST CUTTING GUIDE

Year	Stand	Total Acres	Acres To Cut	Method of Cut	Pulpwood Cubic Feet		Sawlogs Cubic Feet		Comments
					SW	HW	SW	HW	
'79	(2)	84	24	FIRST CUT OF 3-STAGE SHELTERWOOD	2430	2160	10,530	2160	REMOVE 15% FROM SOFTWOODS; 20% FROM HARDWOODS
'80	(8)	15	2	SALVAGE BLOWDOWNS ON WESTERN EDGE	974	650	4,876	—	
'81	(2)	84	30	FIRST CUT OF 3-STAGE SHELTERWOOD	3038	2700	13,163	2700	SAME AS ABOVE ('79)
'83	(2)	84	30	FIRST CUT OF 3-STAGE SHELTERWOOD	3038	2700	13,163	2700	SAME AS ABOVE ('79)
'85	(5)	17	8	CLEARCUT	16,384	—	1824	—	IMMATURE STAND UNDER SEC. 9 – FOREST IMPROV. ACT. GET PERMISSION FROM BOARD TO CLEARCUT. MAY HAVE TO BE PLANTED IF NATURAL REGENERATION INADEQUATE.

TABLE 4: FIVE YEAR SILVICULTURE GUIDE

Year	Stand	Acres	Acres to Treat	Treatment	Comments
EVERY YEAR	(1)	37	37	THINNING & SELECTION CUTTING TO DEVELOP MAPLE SUGARBUSH.	SEE MANUAL. WOOD CUT SHOULD BE USED FOR FUELWOOD.
'79	(10)	22	22	PREPARE SITE FOR PLANTING WITH PLOW. PLANT IN STRIPS IN 1980.	WORK SHOULD BE DONE IN FALL OF 1979, FOR PLANTING IN SPRING OF 1980.
'80	(10)	22	22	PLANT 26,000 WHITE SPRUCE (6X6 SPACING)	
'80	(3)	3	3	PLANT 3,600 RED PINE (6X6 SPACING)	DON'T PLANT WITHIN 20 FEET OF THE ROAD. CHECK NEED FOR SITE PREPARATION.
'80	(4)	34	34	CLEANING TO FAVOUR RED SPRUCE AND WHITE PINE.	

TABLE 5: FIVE YEAR GUIDE FOR ROADS, BOUNDARY LINES AND FIRE PONDS

Year	Road Construction	Boundary Lines	Ponds
1980 – 83	*0.6 MILE MAIN ROAD* *0.25 MILE EXTRACTION ROAD*	—	—
BEFORE 1984	————	*0.5 MILE RE-MARKING ONLY.*	—
1985	————	————	*1 POND*

TABLE 6: FIVE YEAR WOODLAND MANAGEMENT PROGRESS REPORT

Roads / Silviculture — Years	1	2	3	4	5	Total
Miles const.						
Cost						
Gravelled Miles						
Cost						
A. Total Cost						
Site Preparation						
Cost						
Planting (acres)						
Cost						
Cleaning (acres)						
Cost						
Thinning (acres)						
Cost						
Other (acres)						
Cost						
B. Total Cost						

Ponds / Boundaries — Years	1	2	3	4	5	Total
Number						
C. Total Cost						
Miles Estab.						
D. Total Cost						
All Costs A, B, C, D						

Harvesting — Years	1 SW	1 HW	2 SW	2 HW	3 SW	3 HW	4 SW	4 HW	5 SW	5 HW	Total SW	Total HW
Cubic Feet												
Revenue												
Cubic Feet												
Revenue												
Others ( )												
Revenue												
Total Revenue												

Appendix V

Things to Consider in a Contract for Sale of Wood

A timber sale contract is a legally binding document governing the terms of a timber sale. Verbal agreements may cause seller and buyer dissatisfaction and loss of trust. A good written contract protects both the seller and buyer from legal problems arising from the harvest and sale of forest products.

An effective timber sale contract should include:

1 *Names and addresses of seller and buyer*

2 *Documentation of seller's ownership and right to sell forest products*

3 *Exact location and description of the area* - The description should cover the sale area. The acreage and the method and responsibility of marking the trees or the sale area boundary should be included.

4 *Timber bought and sold* - The wording must designate the forest products sold as marked trees or on the basis of volume by species. If required, include unit of measure (cords, cubic feet, board feet, or weight), log rule, method and place of scaling. The contract should indicate the price and location, and the person responsible for scaling.

5 *Price basis and methods and terms of payment* - Forest products may be sold for a lump sum or on value per unit basis (such as dollars per thousand board feet). The price basis, method and time of payment, and the time of sale must be understood by both parties.

6 *Financial responsibility of the buyer* - The seller should make sure that the buyer carries personal liability insurance, property damage insurance, and Workmen's Compensation Insurance during the life of the contract. To ensure performance, the buyer may be required to produce a performance or guarantee bond.

7 *Duration of agreement (time limit)* - Provisions for or against extending time limits may also be included.

8 *Conditions governing removal* - Generalities are worthless. Clauses restricting the manner and methods of harvesting must be specific. Too often useless wording is employed such as "perform in a workmanlike manner" or "the timber shall be cut in accordance with sound forestry practices." Rather than state "the buyer agrees to cause no unnecessary damage to fences, roads or fields of the seller, and agrees to restore them to the same state of repair if he does cause any damage," it would be far better to write "the buyer agrees that in the event fences are cut or broken he will immediately repair them effectively and prevent

the escape of any livestock contained therein, and he agrees to restore the existing roads of the seller to a state or condition at least equal to that now existing."

Other conditions to include are: equipment limitations — are multifunction processors to be allowed — where and how branches, tops and stumps are to be left, provisions for buyer's right to enter and leave the property, responsibility for damage to other property by fire or negligence; and that all cutting must comply with the provisions of the Forest Improvement Act.

9 *Conditions governing utilization* - Include stump heights, minimum lengths and diameter of merchantable material.

10 *Ownership of by-products* - Slabs, shavings, chips, stumps, and sawdust are saleable in some areas. Ownership disputes may develop during the life of the contract.

11 *Provision for or against assignment of the contract* - If the seller definitely wants the party with whom he negotiates to be responsible for performance, he will forbid assignment of the contract in whole or in part. On the other hand, an assignable contract will sometimes command a higher price for the forest products and it might be to the advantage of the seller to grant this right. When assignment is permitted, the buyer will sometimes agree to be fully responsible for performance even though he sells his interest in the forest products to another.

12 *Clause for arbitration* - Generally, in the case of disagreement, each party to the contract names one person and they agree on a third to settle disputes arising under this contract.

13 *Signature of all parties*

14 *Notarization*

Appendix VI

Tables of Measures

The basic metric units of measure are:

length	- metre
area	- square metre, hectare
volume (solid)	- cubic metre
volume (liquid)	- litre
weight	- gram

Prefixes to these basic units designate smaller or larger measures:

milli	- 1/1000
centi	- 1/100
deci	- 1/10
deca	- 10
hecto	- 100
kilo	- 1000

Examples:

millimetre	- 1/1000 of a metre
kilometre	- 1000 metres

and similarly for:

millilitre and milligram
kilolitre and kilogram

Symbols (abbreviations)

ENGLISH   METRIC

Length

inch	— in	millimetre	— mm
foot	— ft	centimetre	— cm
yard	— yd	decimetre	— dm
link	— lk	metre	— m
chain	— ch	decametre	— dam
mile	— mi	hectometre	— hm
		kilometre	— km

Area

square inch	— sq in	square millimetre	— mm^2
square foot	— sq ft		
square yard	— sq yd	square metre	— m^2
square chain	— sq ch		
milacre	— milacre	square kilometre	— km^2
acre	— ac	hectare	— ha
square mile	— sq mi		

Volume (Solid)

cubic inch	— cu in	cubic millimetre	— mm^3
cubic foot	— cu ft		
cubic yard	— cu yd	cubic metre	— m^3
cunit	— cu		
cord	— cd		
foot board measure	— fbm		

Measures and Conversions

ENGLISH			METRIC		
Length					
1 foot	=	12 inches	1 centimetre	=	10 millimetres
1 yard	=	3 feet	1 metre	=	100 centimetres
1 chain	=	66 feet	1 kilometre	=	1000 metres
1 chain	=	100 links			
1 mile	=	80 chains			
1 mile	=	5280 feet			

Conversions					
1 inch	=	2.54 centimetres	1 centimetre	=	0.3937 inch
1 foot	=	0.3048 metre	1 metre	=	3.2808 feet
1 yard	=	0.9144 metre		=	1.0936 yards
1 chain	=	20.1168 metres		=	0.0497 chain
1 mile	=	1.6093 kilometres	1 kilometre	=	0.6214 mile

ENGLISH

Area

1 square foot	=	144 square inches
1 square yard	=	9 square feet
1 milacre	=	43.56 square feet
1 acre	=	1,000 milacres
	=	43,560 square feet
	=	10 square chains
1 square mile	=	640 acres

Conversions

1 square inch	=	6.4516 square centimetres
1 square foot	=	0.0929 square metre
1 milacre	=	4.0469 square metres
1 acre	=	0.4047 hectare
1 square mile	=	2.590 square kilometres

METRIC

Area

1 square centimetre	=	100 square millimetres
1 square metre	=	10,000 square centimetres
1 hectare	=	10,000 square metres
1 square kilometre	=	100 hectares

Conversions

1 square centimetre	=	0.155 square inch
1 square metre	=	10.7639 square feet
	=	0.2471 milacre
1 hectare	=	2.471 acres
1 square kilometre	=	0.3861 square mile

ENGLISH

Volume (Solid)

1 cubic foot	=	1728 cubic inches
1 cubic yard	=	27 cubic feet
1 cunit	=	100 cubic feet (solid wood)
1 cord	=	128 cubic feet (stacked wood)
1 cubic foot	=	12 feet board measure

METRIC

1 cubic centimetre	=	1,000 cubic millimetres
1 cubic metre	=	1,000,000 cubic centimetres

Conversions

1 cubic inch	=	16.3871 cubic centimetres
1 cubic foot	=	0.0283 cubic metre
1 cubic yard	=	0.7645 cubic metre
1 cunit	=	2.8317 cubic metres (solid wood)
1 cord (stacked wood)	=	3.6245 cubic metres (stacked wood)
1000 feet board measure	=	2.3597 cubic metres (theoretical)
1 cubic centimetre	=	0.061 cubic inch
1 cubic metre	=	35.3147 cubic feet
	=	1.3079 cubic yards
	=	0.3531 cunit
	=	423.7764 feet board measure (theoretical)

Volume (Liquid)

1 gallon	=	4.5459 litres
1 litre	=	0.2199 gallon

ENGLISH		METRIC	
Weight			
1 pound	= 16 ounces	1 centigram	= 10 milligrams
1 short ton	= 2000 pounds	1 gram	= 100 centigrams
		1 kilogram	= 1000 grams
		1 metric ton or tonne	= 1000 kilograms

Conversions			
1 ounce	= 28.3495 grams	1 gram	= 0.0353 ounce
1 pound	= 0.4536 kilogram	1 kilogram	= 2.2046 pounds
1 short ton	= 0.9072 tonne	1 tonne	= 1.1023 short tons
			= 2204.623 pounds

Proportion (Ratio): Area Basis

Numbers

1 per square foot	=	10.7639 per square metre
1 per square metre	=	0.0929 per square foot
1 per milacre	=	0.2471 per square metre
1 per square metre	=	4.0469 per milacre
1 per acre	=	2.4711 per hectare
1 per hectare	=	0.4047 per acre
1 per square mile	=	0.3861 per square kilometre
1 per square kilometre	=	2.5899 per square mile

Area

1 square foot per acre	=	0.2296 square metre per hectare
1 square metre per hectare	=	4.356 square feet per acre

Volume (Solid)

1 cubic foot per acre	=	0.0699 cubic metre per hectare
1 cubic metre per hectare	=	14.2913 cubic feet per acre
1 cunit per acre	=	6.9972 solid cubic metres per hectare
1 solid cubic metre per hectare	=	0.1429 cunit per acre
1 stacked cord per acre	=	8.9565 stacked cubic metres per hectare
1 stacked cubic metre per hectare	=	0.1116 stacked cord per acre

Additional Reading:

CANADIAN STANDARDS ASSOCIATION. *Metric Practice Guide.* Ottawa, Ontario: National Standards of Canada. CAN-3-001-02-73. 1973.

Appendix VII

Desirable Stocking After Thinning

Desired DBH at Harvest	Number of Trees Per Acre		
	Softwood	Mixedwood	Hardwood
6″	1137	853	569
7″	857	643	429
8″	671	503	336
9″	541	405	270
10″	446	334	223
11″	374	281	187
12″	319	239	159
13″	275	207	138
14″	240	180	120
15″	212	159	106
16″	188	141	94
17″	168	126	84
18″	152	114	76
19″	137	103	69
20″	125	94	62

Glossary of Terms

Accessibility
The ease with which standing timber can be felled and extracted.

Age
The number of annual growth rings between the bark and the centre of the tree at breast height (breast height age) at stump height (stump age).

Age Class
The interval into which the age range of trees, stands or forests is divided.

All-aged
Applied to a stand in which trees of all ages up to and including those of the felling age are found.

Alkaline soil
Any soil showing an alkaline reaction or with a pH greater than 7.

Allowable cut
The amount of wood which may be harvested under management for a given period (annually or periodically) from a specified area.

Annual ring
The layer of wood produced by the growth of a single year which in cross section appears as an annual ring. The spring wood of faster growth is light. The summer wood of slower growth is darker, harder and stronger.

Aspect
The direction towards which a slope faces.

Barren
Land that bears no trees or only stunted trees.

Basal area
The area in square feet (square metres) of the cross section at breast height of a single tree or of all the trees in an acre (hectare).

Board foot
A measure equal to $1'' \times 12'' \times 12''$.

Bog
A wet, low area, often an old lake bed, filling or filled with partially decayed matter.

Bole
See stem.

Breast height
4.5 feet (1.3 metres) above the average ground level.

Brow
A landing or yard at the edge of a road or river, where forest products are sorted and made ready for another form of transport.

Browse
To eat the twigs and leaves of woody plants. Deer, moose and rabbits are browsers.

Brush
Shrubs and short scrubby tree species that do not reach merchantable size.

Callus
Tissue laid down by the tree at the edges of a wound or around the stub of a dead branch.

Cambium
Is a narrow zone of cells lying between the inner bark and the sapwood. It is the growth layer which produces new bark and new wood.

Canker

An area of diseased tissue, often discolored and cracked, on a living branch or stem. May be annual, with new tree growth covering the wound quickly, or perennial, where disease growth prevents tree growth from covering the wound.

Canopy

The cover of branches and foliage formed by tree crowns.

Cleaning

A cutting made in a stand not past the sapling stage, to free the best trees from undersirable individuals of the same age and size which overtop them or are likely to do so or to reduce stocking to a recommended level.

Clearcutting

Strictly clearcutting is the removal of the entire standing tree crop. In practice, it may refer to exploitation that leaves much unsaleable material standing — commercial clearcutting.

Climax

The culminating stage of a natural forest succession for a given environment, the vegetation having reached a highly stable condition. Sugar maple, yellow birch, beech and hemlock are considered to be climax species. Such species are shade tolerant.

Condominant trees

Trees with crowns forming the general level of the crown cover and receiving full light from above but comparatively little from the sides usually with medium sized crowns more or less crowded on the sides.

Community, forest

All the plants and animals in a particular habitat that are bound together by food chains and other interrelationships.

Cord, standard

A stack of wood containing 128 cubic feet.

Crook

A defect in logs or trees consisting of an abrupt bend.

Crop tree

Crop tree is any tree forming, or selected to form, part of the final harvest — generally a tree selected in an immature stand for carrying through to the final harvest.

Crown

The branches and foliage of a tree.

Crown canopy

The more or less continuous cover of branches and foliage formed collectively by the crowns of trees.

Crown closure

The percent of ground area covered by the vertically projected tree crown areas.

Cruise

A survey to locate and estimate the quantity of timber on a given area according to species, size, quality, possible products or other characteristics.

Cull

A tree or log of merchantable size, rendered unmerchantable because of poor form, limbiness, rot, or other defect.

Cunit

100 cubic feet of solid wood.

Cutting cycle

The planned interval between major felling operations in the same stand.

Decadence

Deterioration, degeneration of trees and stands due to age.

Decay

The decomposition of wood substance by fungi.

Defect

Any irregularity or imperfection in a tree or log that reduces the volume of sound wood or value of the log.

Density, stand
Is an indicator of how well the site is occupied by trees. Expressed as basal area per acre, it is a measure of the portion of an acre occupied by stems. Expressed as percent of crown closure, it is an estimate of how well the site is used.

Desirable species
All species stated in the Forest Improvement Act and such other species which the Board subsequently includes as desirable species for any District.

Desirable stand
A stand having more than 50 percent of its merchantable volume in healthy desirable species.

Diameter at breast height
The diameter of a tree, outside bark at 4.5 feet (1.3 metres) above average ground level.

Diameter limit
The smallest size to which trees are to be cut. Differs from species to species and is measured 1 foot (30 centimetres) above average ground level outside bark.

Dibble
A tool for hand planting tree seedlings.

Dieback
Progressive dying from the extremity of any part of a plant which may or may not result in its total death.

Dominant trees
Trees with crowns extending above the general level of the crown cover and receiving full light from above and partly from the side; they will be larger than the average trees in the stand, and with crowns well developed but possibly somewhat crowded on the sides.

Dot grid
A transparent sheet of film with systematically arranged dots, each dot representing a number of area units (acres, hectares).

Double needled
Also double-foliaged. A term describing balsam fir Christmas trees. "Single-needled" trees have flat foliage. "Double-needled" trees have branches with foliage full and rounded on top.

Ecology
The study of the relations of living things to one another and to their environment.

Ecoregion
A region that differs from another region by specific ecological conditions.

Ecosystem
All living things and their environment in an area of any size that we isolate for study. All the living things are linked together by energy and food flow.

Ericaceous
Describing a family of shrubs or bushes popularly known as health plants — Ericaceae.

Even-aged
Applied to a stand in which relatively small age differences exist between individual trees.

Fauna
The animal life

Forest
A complex community of plants and animals in which stands of trees are the most conspicuous members.

Forest Management
The practical application of scientific, economic and social principles to the administration of a forest property for specified objectives.

Girdling
To encircle the stem of a living tree with cuts that completely sever bark and cambium and often are carried well into the outer sapwood, for the purpose of killing the tree by preventing the passage of nutrients.

Group selection
A modification of the selection method whereby the mature timber is removed in small groups rather than by single trees.

Habitat
The natural home or environment of a plant or animal.

Herbaceous
Describing seed producing plants that do not develop persistent woody tissue above ground. Includes herbs and grasses.

Highgrading
Selective cutting, a type of exploitation cutting that removes certain species, above a certain size, and of high value with sustained yields being wholly or largely ignored or found impossible to fulfill.

Hummock
A hillock or mound.

Increment
The increase in girth, diameter, basal area, height, volume, quality or value of individual trees or crops. Refers mainly to past radial increase as measured from the annual growth rings. Current annual is for a given year. Mean annual is the average annual for the total age.

Instar
The form assumed by an insect during a particular stage in its larval development which is initiated and/or terminated by the shedding of its skin.

Intermediate trees
Trees with crowns below, but still extending into the general level of the forest canopy, receiving a little direct light from above, but none from the sides; these trees usually have small crowns that are shaded on all sides.

Internode
The length of stem between two nodes, where leaves or branches arise.

Intolerant species
Those trees which cannot persist under the shade of other trees.

Larva
An immature insect that emerges from the egg differing in form from the adult into which it develops via the pupal stage. Worm is a loose colloquial synonym. It is usually the stage in the life cycle of an insect that does the most damage to forest trees.

Loam
A non-sandy, non-sticky, friable soil, intermediate in texture and properties between fine-textured and coarse-textured soils.

Lean
Referring to a tree not standing straight.

Overmature
The period in its life cycle when a tree or stand is in decline in growth and/or value.

Peavey
A stout wooden lever fitted into a tapered metal socket terminating in a steel spike and carrying towards its upper end a hinged steel hook or dog. It is used mainly in turning and handling logs. The cant hook differs in that the metal socket terminates in a projection (various patterns) facing the hook to provide the countergrip.

Pioneer species
A plant capable of invading bare sites and persisting there until supplanted by succession species. They usually promote the establishment of more exacting species. Poplar, aspen, white birch and willow are pioneer species.

Pole

A young tree, from the time its lower branches begin to die, up to the time when its rate of height growth begins to slow down and crown expansion becomes marked. The tree has a diameter at breast height of not less than 4 in. (10 cm) and not more than 8 in (20 cm).

Pruning

The removal of live or dead branches from a standing tree.

Pulpwood

Wood cut and prepared primarily for manufacture into wood pulp.

Pupa

An immature, generally immobile, insect stage between larva and adult.

Radial suppression

The process whereby growth on a side of a tree stem is reduced (suppressed) because of competition with its neighbours.

Reforestation

The artificial establishment of forest on an area.

Refractometer

An instrument for measuring the passage of light and used to determine the sugar content in maple syrup.

Regeneration

The process by which a forest is renewed.

Root collar

The transition zone between stem and root.

Rotation

The period of years required to establish and grow timber crops to a specified condition of maturity for regeneration cutting — from harvest cut to harvest cut.

Roundwood

Wood in the round — before being processed.

Sandvik hoe

A specially designed hoe for planting tree seedlings.

Sapling

A young tree no longer a seedling but not yet a pole, i.e. greater than 3 ft. (metre) tall but less than 3.6 in. (9 cm) in diameter at breast height.

Sapwood

The living wood of pale colour next to the bark. The sapwood is the wood first formed by the cambium. It conducts mineral solutions from the roots to the leaves, and serves for food storage.

Sawlog

A log considered suitable in size and quality for producing sawn timber.

Sawtimber

Trees suitable in size and quality for producing sawlogs.

Scarify

To break up the forest floor and topsoil preparatory to regeneration.

Scrub growth

Inferior growth consisting of small or stunted trees or shrubs of low economic potential.

Seed year

In respect of any species, particularly trees of irregular or infrequent seed production, the year in which it produces, either as an individual or as a stand, an adequate amount of seed. Many periodic seeders produce heavy ("bumper") crops during their seed years.

Selection cutting

The periodic removal of trees, individually or in small groups (group selection) from an uneven-aged forest in order to realize the yield and establish a new crop of irregular constitution. The improvement of the forest is a primary consideration.

202

Selective cutting
See high-grading.

Shelterbelt
A strip of living trees and/or shrubs maintained mainly to provide shelter from wind, snowdrift, sun, etc. under some conditions may be called a windbreak.

Shelterwood cutting
Any regeneration cutting in a more or less regular and mature stand, designed to establish a new stand under the protection of the old. Shelterwood system, an even-aged silvicultural system in which, in order to provide a source of seed and/or protection for regeneration, the old stand (the Shelterwood) is removed in two or more successive shelterwood cuttings, the first of which is ordinarily the seed cutting (though it may be preceded by a preparatory cutting) and the last is the final cutting, any intervening cuttings being termed removal cutting. The lengths of the regeneration interval and the regeneration period determine the degree of uniformity in age of the resulting stand.

Silviculture
The science and art of cultivating forest crops. More particularly, the theory and practice of controlling the establishment, composition, constitution and growth of forests.

Site
An area, considered as to its ecological factors with reference to capacity to produce forests or other vegetation; the combination of biotic, climatic and soil conditions of an area.

Snag
A standing dead tree from which most of the leaves and most of the branches have fallen.

Sod scalper
An attachment to a tree planting machine to scrape or scalp sod away from the planted trees.

Sprout
Any shoot arising from above ground level usually from a stump or stem.

Stagnant
Stands in which growth and development have all but ceased due to poor site and/or overstocking.

Stand
A community, particularly of trees, possessing sufficient uniformity as regards composition, constitution, age, spatial arrangement or condition, to be distinguishable from adjacent communities, so forming a silvicultural or management entity.

Stem
The trunk or bole of a tree.

Stocking
The number of trees per acre.

Stumpage
The value of timber as it stands uncut in the forest. Standing value.

Sucker
Any shoot arising from below ground level usually from a root.

Suppressed trees
Trees with their crowns entirely below the general forest canopy which receive no direct light either from above or from the sides.

Sustained yield
Implies continuous production with the aim of achieving an approximate balance between net growth and harvest.

Thinning
Cutting in an immature stand to improve quality, to improve species composition, to obtain greater merchantable yield, and to recover material that may be lost otherwise.

Tolerant species
Those trees which can persist and grow, perhaps slowly, under shade of other trees.

Type

A descriptive term used to identify areas of similar character as regards composition, development and growth.

Weeding

A cultural operation eliminating or suppressing undesirable vegetation during the initial period of a plantation.

Whorl

One year's growth of lateral branches.

Windfirm

Trees able to stand strong winds — to resist windfall.

Windthrow

A tree or trees uprooted by the wind.

Wolf tree

A vigorous tree, generally of bad growth form, that occupies more growing space than its value warrants, so harming, or threatening to harm, potentially better neighbours. It is generally a dominant or codominant tree with a large spreading crown.

Veneer log

A log considered suitable in size and quality for producing veneer.

Viburnum

A group of wood shrubs or bushes, such as highbush cranberry, hobble bush, withe-rod.

INDEX